Jump Start

Jump Start

AJ Hackett
with Winston Aldworth

RANDOM HOUSE
NEW ZEALAND

National Library of New Zealand Cataloguing-in-Publication Data

Hackett, A. J. (Alan John), 1958-
Jump start / A.J. Hackett.
ISBN-13: 978-1-86941-842-7
ISBN-10: 1-86941-842-5
1. Hackett, A. J. (Alan John), 1958- 2. Businessmen—New
Zealand—Biography. 3. Entrepreneurship—New Zealand.
4. Bungee jumping. 5. Extreme sports. I. Title.
338.04092—dc 22

A RANDOM HOUSE BOOK
published by
Random House New Zealand
18 Poland Road, Glenfield, Auckland, New Zealand

www.randomhouse.co.nz

First published 2006

ISBN 13: 978 1 86941 842 7
ISBN 10: 1 86941 842 5

Cover design: Matt Smith, Pavlov's Dog Design, Cairns
Page design: Sharon Grace, Grace Design, Auckland
Printed in China by Everbest Printing Co

To my amazing kids —
Dean, Jayde and my gorgeous Margaux.
Thank you for your love and patience.

Contents

Bridge. It was a 19-metre drop into the blue of Auckland's Waitemata Harbour. The air rushed up past my face and I braced to hit the water when suddenly I had the most amazing sensation — I felt the pull of the rubber cord attached to my back, courtesy of a borrowed parachute harness. As it halted my fall, my head and limbs lurched forward; then, when I was only a couple of metres clear of the water, the cord twanged me back up again. I roared with exhilaration, my feet frantically flailing about in mid-air.

For a moment, as I launched back upwards, I wondered if my head was about to clatter into the underside of the bridge. But, thankfully, my momentum ran short a couple of metres clear of the bridge and then I was falling again. I'd never felt anything like this — I wriggled around and laughed my head off as I yo-yoed beneath the Greenhithe Bridge. I had just done my first bungy jump. Bouncing up and down and looping about on this fantastic rubber cord — it's fair to say I was sold on the idea right from the outset.

Once I had stopped yahooing and managed to quieten down a bit, my friend Chris Sigglekow yelled down to me from above: 'Whaddaya reckon?'

'I wanna go again! Mate, this is unreal! I love it!'

Chris lowered me down a little towards the water so I could slip out of the harness. It was mid-November 1986, and the waters of the Waitemata were still pretty cold, despite it being a sunny day. As I swam the 30 metres to shore, I looked back over my shoulder and watched the cord flickering upward as Chris pulled it in so that we could get it ready for another jump. I was absolutely stoked. I was already wondering what else we could jump off — but how far would that cord stretch before it simply broke? Chris and I each took two jumps that day. Being adventurous but not suicidal, we had chosen a bridge we knew we could jump from safely with enough water to make for a reasonable splashdown if the bungy cord didn't do exactly what we were hoping it would. But it had worked fine — in fact it had worked an absolute charm.

It was Chris who first brought the idea of bungy jumping into New Zealand. In the early 1980s, he'd heard about some Oxford University students who'd pulled a similar stunt off a bridge near Bristol, in England. So one Christmas when he was down near Nelson in the South Island, he thought he'd give it a go himself. With the same borrowed parachute harness that later got a workout off the Greenhithe Bridge, a bit of cord cut to a fairly random length and an understanding of knots that was more enthusiastic than informed, Chris flung himself off the Pelorus Bridge. This was in January 1980, six years before he and I did the jump at Greenhithe. Chris' leap from the Pelorus Bridge didn't quite work out — he went straight into the water, feet first and pretty much at full speed before the cord took his weight. The cord then ripped him out of the water — a sodden and excited mess — and twanged him about.

He was left soaked and with some pretty impressive bruises from where the parachute webbing had dug into his torso, but it didn't dampen his enthusiasm. The jump from the Pelorus was ten metres or so and plenty of local kids leaped off the bridge unaided for kicks. Chris laughed it off and packed the parachute away in a wardrobe where it gathered dust until 1986 when he told me about his bid to become some sort of antipodean Icarus.

Once he put the whole crazy idea to me, it captivated me immediately. I was a typical Kiwi male in his mid-twenties — a bit of an adventure buff, into my rock climbing, speed skiing, surfing and anything else that involved initiative and exhilaration. Chris rightly figured I'd be the kind of bloke who would be keen to try out something as crazy as bouncing off a bridge held up by an elastic band. Over a beer, Chris talked me through what was involved. The mechanics of it — the harness, rubber, knots and ties — all seemed simple enough, and the rush from the jump would clearly be fantastic. We discussed our options for jumping: where we would jump from and where we would get the rubber. Gradually we went from talking in hypotheticals to planning the first session at the Greenhithe Bridge.

I was enthusiastic and enough of an adrenalin junkie to be drawn to the idea in principle, but I also had something extra that was to prove crucial to the future of the whole exercise — I knew my ropes really well. My experience rock climbing meant that I could tie the knots that would mean we would be safe when the cord took our weight. Right from the first jump I did, I wanted to know how to do things safely and how to make the process of falling and bouncing back up as predictable as possible. And if we couldn't make it all predictable, then we'd drop it because even back then I didn't like pain and I didn't like the idea of being responsible for inflicting it on others.

Chris had organised a basic study with people at the University of Auckland, which established some safe working loads for the rubber cords. They told us that a single strand of the rubber cord would break when it was extended to 6.7 times its length, while at four times its length it would be at only 15 per cent of its breaking strain, which gave us a massive safety margin. And it gave us a general formula: divide the height of the jump by four and that determines the length of your bungy cord. After establishing that, it was just a question of how thick to make the bungy cord for the different weights of your jumpers.

So we already had a reasonable understanding of the material we were working with and its theoretical capabilities. We just needed to test it on ourselves to prove this theory. Chris and I got some rubber cord from a company called Kinnears, which produced ropes and 'stretchies' for the yachting industry which, of course, was becoming really huge in Auckland.

On Sunday morning, 23 November 1986, we drove out to the Greenhithe Bridge with a box full of rubber strands, a bunch of karabiners, the parachute harness and a few odds and sods. I'd had a look at the bridge a week or so before to suss it all out and design the mechanics of the rigging system and, of course, to make sure we could do it without whacking into the bridge's uprights or hidden rocks beneath the water.

We laid out the cord under the bridge, out of sight from passers-by. It came as thin strands bound up in a heavy roll. We measured out how much we wanted and pretty much just folded it back over itself to make a thick, strong cord — a bungy. I set up a simple rigging system using some of my climbing gear and fixed it onto the handrail of the bridge.

Nineteen metres is a manageable little drop into deep water so, if anything went majorly wrong, we'd just go for a swim. All the same, we had a fairly scientific testing method ready to go: that is to say, we took an old punch bag, stuffed it full of rusty diving belts and weights and chucked it over the side of the bridge to see what would happen. Okay, so maybe it wasn't entirely scientific. I was about 65 kg and Chris was about 70 kg and we filled the bag to match our weights and threw it off the edge of the bridge.

Chris worked in television production, and he'd brought a friend along with some borrowed gear to film the tests and the jumps. We watched the footage of the tests and it all seemed pretty sound. The punch bag just cleared the water and bounced back — nothing broke. Great. We even did a second test just to make sure . . . so when it came time for us to jump ourselves, we had no fear at all, as we'd seen it work with the punch bag and felt confident about not hitting the water hard. If nothing else, I figured the cord would slow me down before it failed, so at worst I would have a feet-first equivalent of a ten-metre drop into the water. And, as I said, it worked like a charm for both of us.

Of course there are variables — on that very first day, we learnt that you can't take anything for granted with bungy. My worry about slamming into the underside of the bridge became a bruising reality for Chris when he knocked into it on the rebound during his second jump. Thankfully no major damage was done — it was just a little knock. That was the first of many minor surprises, but it did highlight to me the fact that we needed to figure out a lot more of the science behind the cords.

The feeling after my first bungy jump? Pretty much the same as people all over the world who do their first bungy — completely stoked. Anyone who's done a bungy knows it takes a hell of a long time to wipe the smile away and it can be a life-changing, positive experience. We went home feeling pretty chuffed with ourselves and watched the video footage from the day's activities over a couple of beers, which again is pretty much exactly what people do today after a jump.

As for that countdown, I figured that as I used to do one when I was jumping off things without a rubber band, it made sense to use one for this exercise. At AJ Hackett Bungy sites around the world today, we still use the countdown to give jumpers that little bit of extra help in getting off the platform and, more importantly, to make everyone focus on whether it is all clear and safe to jump.

The next weekend we went down to Hamilton to jump off one of the really high bridges down there. They've got some beautiful bridges, right in the middle of the city, spanning the Waikato River. A couple of mates were in Auckland — Henry van Asch and Martin Jones — and they came down with us. Chris and I went through the same Greenhithe Bridge routine — we measured the height of the bridge, agreed on the rigging system, then built the cord on site and did a couple of tests with the punch bag, before going over the side ourselves.

There I am standing up on the ledge of the bridge, about 100 metres from the main drag of central Hamilton and about 30-odd metres (vertically) from the surface of the Waikato River. I've got a pretty pumped expression on my face and I'm wearing a parachute harness — and that's when the cops pull up. I must have looked a right nutter.

Naturally, a bit of a crowd had built up so the passing cop car had pulled over to see what the fuss was about. This was the bungy crew's first experience with the law and I really had no idea what they would make of us, but I had a little plan.

'Leave the talking to me, guys,' I whispered through a clenched smile as two policemen hopped out of their patrol car and walked over.

'G'day fellas, what's going on here?'

How do you begin to explain? I couldn't just say: 'Well, officer, we're reinventing adventure tourism.' But I had a simple plan ready in case the police showed an interest in what we were doing — I offered them a jump. I told them a little about this new-fangled entertainment we were trying out and made my pitch.

predictable at 20–40 metres. I knew how it dropped and how it would rebound. But I wanted to test the limits a bit. There were some pretty major unknowns. How long does a bungy cord last? What affects it? Does it vary at height? Does the way you jump make a difference? How much space do you need to allow for rebounds? We were very much in the dark.

I hoped to find a couple of answers without meeting the river bed, 80-odd bloody metres below. That was the first time I really contended with the whole issue of mortality — but I'd tied the knots and tested the equipment myself, so I had confidence in the system. The rest was blind faith. That big jump was glorious — it was my first major rebound. What a summer!

One day we were jumping the South Rangitikei Viaduct and a train came by just as we were getting set to do our jumps. We all ducked down and tucked into the side of the viaduct as it shunted past us. This thing lumbers along and there was this old Maori bloke, a railways worker, standing at the back of the last carriage smoking a cigarette and admiring the views. He's standing there in his own little world, and then we all come into view as the train goes by and he's just staring at us, and we're all staring up at him, with our bungy ropes over our shoulders and me in a parachute harness. It was one of those really surreal wee moments that life throws your way.

I was due to fly out for France with Henry and a couple of other mates to represent New Zealand on the European speed skiing circuit, so Chris and I planned a quality farewell for the day I was hopping on the plane — 6 February 1987. The pair of us, along with my friend Rob Foreman and a friend of Chris's, planned to jump off the Auckland Harbour Bridge. We went through the same secret squirrel routine of getting out onto the platform beneath the bridge at first light. Our two friends jumped first, with Chris and me manning the lines. We lowered them into the water where they got into another friend's boat.

Just like the last time we jumped the Harbour Bridge, the sun was starting to play across the water. Chris and I were sitting on the platform sorting out our kit and talking about what a great summer we'd had. I was going over with a foot rigging and Chris was in the trusty old parachute harness.

We stood up ready to make our valedictory jumps to mark the end of a great summer, when suddenly a voice booms out: 'Do not jump. We advise you not to jump.'

We had company. The Auckland police boat — the old *Deodar* — puttered out into the half-light, just beneath the bridge. Bloody Waitemata Harbour Baywatch were on the scene, just as I was about to launch on my au revoir bungy. Someone must have tipped them off. Chris and I are standing there trussed up like turkeys and all pumped up for our final jump together.

I looked over to Chris and said: 'Whaddaya reckon? We're bloody caught either way. We can pack up the gear and walk up top where the cops will bust us, or we can get one more sweet jump in and get busted in the water.'

Of course we jumped. Chris remembers it: 'You went momentarily before me — straight out into your head-first dive — and I saw the coppers' jaws drop. All these police on the back of the *Deodar* must have been thinking they were about to fish dead bodies out of the water.'

What we didn't know at the time was that, as it was a weekday, the police had stopped all the traffic on the bridge above us and there was a massive delay for people getting to work in the city. The police thought that they needed to clear the area to deal with these lunatics jumping off the bridge. Was this some sort of mass suicide attempt? They weren't to know it was just the boys playing with their rubber bands. Suffice to say, we got busted in the water. I got a fantastic water touch — I went in to about my waist.

The police only had two queries for us. 'What's it like?' and 'How much have you been drinking?' (Answers: 'Bloody great' and 'one glass of champagne'.) Not only were the police unsure if we had broken any laws but also, as we had jumped off the middle of the bridge, they were unsure about which side of the harbour we should be processed on — Auckland Central or Takapuna Police Station. While they were making up their minds I was watching the clock tick; I had an awful lot to do in the space of twelve hours. There were wages to be paid to my crew of builders, a building project to be wrapped up, Henry and Martin had to be picked up from the airport, my luggage had to be packed, the television and the local papers all wanted an interview and I had to get onto the 9 pm flight to Europe. Of course, we also had to squeeze in a couple of hours at the pub to celebrate. But first, I had to charm my way out of the police station.

The police were actually pretty cool about it. I had a ticket to fly out of the country that evening so they figured I wouldn't be around to cause any more trouble. As word of what we had been doing travelled — the newspaper reporters wanted stories from us and there was a fair bit of interest brewing — the cops insisted that we do a little television appearance for the evening news saying 'we're the experts, don't try this at home'. Of course this probably succeeded in piquing more interest than in putting people off, but it kept the law happy. After one of the most hectic days imaginable, I dashed for the plane to Europe. Shortly after take-off, the 747's movie screen played that night's evening news and there I was with my bungy mates at the top of the bulletin. What a day.

I've sometimes wondered how Chris must feel about how it all panned out from there on because he was the one who brought bungy to New Zealand; he was the first of any of us to have a crack at this madcap thing. He introduced me to bungy jumping. Back then I was AJ Hackett, builder, not AJ Hackett Bungy. The thing is that it probably would never have caught on if I hadn't become involved — I reckon his bit of rubber and his parachute harness would have lain there gathering dust at the back of some storage shed.

Up until I flew out for France, Chris and I had done everything together. He stayed in New Zealand, and while I was away he bungied off what, at the time, was the highest bridge in the country — the Mohaka Viaduct, near Gisbourne. It was a 97-metre drop, so no mean feat. Later Chris ran a bungy roadshow in the US and these days he's got a television production company, and is a successful businessman in his own right.

Once I left for France, things progressed very rapidly for me. I bungy jumped off the Eiffel Tower in 1987, and there was a massive reaction in New Zealand. Suddenly I was the Kiwi guy who stuck it to the French. Those smug bastards blew up the *Rainbow Warrior* and now here's a Kiwi lad from the North Shore who's taken a bit of attitude back to them. New Zealanders were really happy that someone had given a bit of stick back to the French. Lots of people were after a piece of me. All of a sudden, everyone knew about bungy jumping and everyone associated bungy jumping with AJ Hackett. Fine by me.

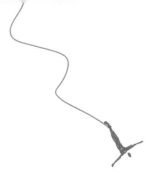

CHAPTER 2

Gumption,
know-how and
selling encyclopedias

T he North Shore was the perfect place for me to grow up. I was born in Pukekohe on 26 May 1958 — eight pounds six ounces, since you ask — but we shifted to the Shore when I was four years old. Our family settled in a little Housing Corporation home at 99 Selwyn Crescent, Milford.

Auckland's North Shore is a sprawling mass of suburbs today but when I was growing up there in the 1960s and 1970s it was largely undeveloped. Down the back of our house, there was a large stand of native bush with a creek running through it and there was a new subdivision being developed up the road. Everything an energetic kid could ask for. The area is all filled in now with masses of housing, but back then it was a wonderland for a young Kiwi kid. I would spend hours with my mates exploring drains in the subdivision and yahooing around on sections with half-built houses.

Me and half a dozen other kids who lived on Selwyn Crescent all built trollies and we would race them on the streets around our houses. There was one particular racing route which those of us in the Trolley Brigade valued highly as proof of a kart's superiority. It involved thundering down a steep slope right outside our house, taking a blind corner — possibly into on-coming traffic — and lurching off down Selwyn Crescent, all the while watching for parked cars. It was pretty much a death trap and, naturally, my kart was the fastest — but only when I was at the controls.

It was a fantastic physical environment for a young fella, but sadly when I was growing up I didn't have a great relationship with my father, Jack Hackett. He was an Aussie fella, hard as nails, brought up in a rural area inland from Townsville. His family had a big cattle station out there; so that was his gig — he was a country boy. Then Mum came along. Joe had been planning on becoming a nun, and had been off travelling for a bit; she had hitchhiked around Europe with some friends, then went and travelled around Australia, largely on her own. She found herself living and working in a place called Cambooya, the real-deal Aussie outback life, with outdoor dunnies and all. It was really bold stuff for a young woman in those days to travel like that. The pair of them met and married. But I think Dad never really felt settled in the land of the Kiwi.

I can't actually remember having anything like a real conversation with my old man, apart from a word or two about the weather and 'pass me the salt' at the dinner table. He seemed a sad old bloke to me. Yet, apparently at work he was the life of the party, the fun of the day — a real good fella. He worked for a company building roads in Auckland, driving rollers and stuff.

At home he was uncommunicative and lonely. Dad had his routines: he'd get up each day at 5.30 am and Mum was up to make him his two hard-boiled eggs. Home at 6.30 pm for a bottle of Lion Red beer. Then, when dinner was ready, one of us would go and get him and we'd eat dinner waiting for him to snap at someone.

Dad allowed this reticent nature to come between us — but it sure as hell showed me how important it is to be there for your kids when it came time for me to have my own. I figure he as good as killed himself too — my father was the only man stubborn enough to commit suicide by skin cancer. Dad was from that macho generation of hard, old antipodean blokes who were as likely to wear sunscreen as they were to don a tutu, and as a result he developed this tumour on the side of his face. Of course he wouldn't go to the doctor about it. It was totally repairable, but being a great stoic he soldiered on, putting plasters on the growth upon his brow, until eventually the skin started to rot, at which point — finally and thankfully — Dad went to the doctor, and they cut out the growth. Three years later, the cancer came back and this time we kids were all a bit older and a bit more strong-willed, so we forced him to see the doctor. But it wasn't easy. He insisted everything was all right, whacking on more plasters and bandages, all the while telling us to mind our own business.

Eventually common sense won. But the situation had become so bad that, when driving my Dad to the hospital, I had to wind down the car window because the stench of rotting flesh from his wound was so strong. What lesson was I meant to learn from my dad's behaviour? Is this what it meant to be manly? Ignoring your family's love and the need for medical help? Once at the hospital, the doctor called me in from the waiting room.

'Mr Hackett, would you like to see what's wrong with your father?' he asked.

I followed the doctor and what I saw alarmed and revolted me. Beneath his bandages Dad had concealed a blackened, rotten piece of flesh the size of a golf ball. This was serious and clearly painful.

'We're going to have to take out his eye and part of his skull,' the doctor said, looking at me as though somehow I had failed by not dragging Dad to the surgery sooner. 'We'll need to take flesh from his arm to put in there.'

Soon after, my dad went in for a ten-hour operation but the tumour had done its damage. Dad never quite healed and quickly faded away, losing half his body weight and dying six months later.

His illness was easily curable. If my dad had communicated with us and been willing to get his tumour looked at when it first appeared, then he could have been with us for years. He could have seen his grandkids grow up and he could have seen my bungy business take off; I could have made him proud. But my Dad missed out on all of that simply because he wouldn't talk.

The lesson that I really learnt from my relationship with my father and the way he died was that you have two choices on this planet: you either live life to the max or you simply exist. Dad simply existed; he let his loneliness beat him down. I swore when he died that I would live life to the max from that moment onwards.

One other useful good thing about my tough relationship with Dad was that it taught me very well about how to deal with what you might call life's difficult personalities. It was a funny upbringing though, having two parents who were so different. With one you were always in a state of stress — every time that person was around, you would be on edge. Then my mum was much more supportive and understanding — and realistic, too. She saw good in all of us kids. She understood that we'd come right, even if we hooned around a bit on the way there.

Cash was often tight when my three sisters — Anna, Elaine and Kitty — and I were growing up. I was the only boy at school whose mum knitted his school uniform jumper because the ones in the shops cost too much. Through necessity, I got right into knitting and sewing myself. I never really wore shoes until I got to intermediate school; but I liked the feeling of being barefoot anyway — to me, running around with the grass between your toes has always been an essential part of the Kiwi upbringing. I sure was an energetic kid, racing around the place barefoot, so of course I had a load of fun at school. I loved lunchtime and sport and hanging about with mates. I often had the old leather belt strapped across my palm for being a bit of a young tearaway, but we never got up to anything too bad.

One time at a parent-teacher night, a teacher said to Mum: 'I've had to discipline AJ a couple of times as he has misbehaved.'

'Give it to him as much as you want,' laughed my mum. 'Give him a clip around the ears if it's necessary!'

Thanks Mum!

As a kid I was never a great scholar, but I enjoyed school and gave it a good crack, going through Campbell's Bay Primary, intermediate at Murray's Bay, and finishing with secondary school at Westlake Boys. I enjoyed the more practical subjects: geography, woodwork, technical drawing and mathematics, which I was pretty good at. Like most Kiwi kids of that era, I was more interested in the outdoor life, and I would always rather play with my mates or head off for a look in the bush up around the back of the house than hit the books or stare at a blackboard. And, of course, I was mad about rugby. I wore some other kid's forehead in my face when I was fifteen, fracturing my cheekbone and landing in a hospital bed for a week, so I missed a heap of crucial exams.

Perhaps one of the reasons I enjoyed playtime at school more than the time spent in the classroom was because I had a little bit of dyslexia. It was nothing major and didn't stop me from reading — to this day I'm a voracious reader — but as a kid I would write a sentence and some of the letters would simply appear in the wrong place. I often felt people in the education system wanted to look down on you. The fact that I was having trouble with writing at school gave them one more reason to pigeonhole me.

It still happens sometimes with my handwriting today. I can look at something and see if it's spelt wrong or whatever but, when it's me writing something, it's a different matter. With handwriting, I just get letters the wrong damn way round. It's like a little block in my head. Once, in the early days when the bungy business was taking off, I wrote out sales reports for all the bungy sites and faxed them out to Helen Farrow, my PA at the time, and some other key staff. I did it in a bit of a hurry and can't have checked over it properly because within minutes my phone was ringing red hot with people calling to ask if I'd been on the booze! As an adult, you can laugh that sort of stuff off, but it's tougher when you're a kid, especially if you don't feel so supported by your teachers. I've got three kids of my own now and I'm thankful they're doing well with their education.

The lack of a lengthy formal education hasn't stopped me from setting up a global industry that has turned over hundreds of millions of dollars. The reality is that education and a nice framed qualification on your wall have very little to do with success in business, and even less to do with success in life — it all depends on how you define success. For me that definition is being happy with what you do; not having $50 million in the bank and rushing off to work every day. When I was growing up, I had some great examples too — I had a grandfather and uncles on my mother's side who were very clever and ran very successful businesses without having a lot of formal education.

These guys were beekeepers and they ran the second-biggest bee-keeping operation in New Zealand, producing over 100 tons of honey a year and exporting queen bees all around the world. It had been a family business for 50 years. These people got pretty wealthy, but did it in a way that meant they still enjoyed their lives, with plenty of trout fishing and lawn bowls. As a kid, I was always amazed by Uncle Donald's huge aviaries filled with unusual birds, and the exotic fish and animals he kept.

For me, these people embodied the best elements of Kiwi society and the ethos that makes us New Zealanders the unique critters that we are. Hard work and ingenuity saw them through tough times in setting up and running their businesses.

My uncle Jim Bates is a classic example. Jim, my mum's brother, didn't get a lot of traditional schooling (there was farm work to be done) and yet he turned out to be one of the most brilliant designers and engineers you could hope to meet. Uncle Jim cracked on to his knack for inventing when his dad had a bumper load of honey on their Taranaki farm and it was going to be a really tough haul to get it all packed away. So Jim — just twelve years old at the time — played around in the toolshed and came up with a honey extractor that helped to speed things up on the farm when they were processing and packing away the honey. It saved his dad a fortune in lost honey from that harvest. Twelve-year-old Jim's invention — the Bates Honey Extractor — came to be a standard tool in the New Zealand beekeeping industry.

He went on to build concrete boats, he also designed and built a boat that was powered by a twelve-metre wind turbine that produced enough energy to maximise the hull speed of the boat. In a world where energy is at a premium and its environmental cost is mounting, I can see that Uncle Jim's inventions were way ahead of their time.

A brilliant man, he was also a warm and friendly uncle. I spent a lot of holidays with Jim and his sons, Peter and John. He was a complete inspiration in terms of coming up with the freakiest ideas and pushing them through to make something special happen — not a million miles away from launching a global bungy-jumping business, you might say. Uncle Jim was a true radical. Totally rejected by the schooling system, it was his mother who taught him to read when he was ten years old.

When Jim's time in Europe was up at the end of the Second World War, he forged a pass and hitched his way around Italy, Greece and Crete. That's the sort of can-do thinking I can really appreciate.

Later in life, the Bates Honey Extractor landed my Uncle Jim one of the most interesting jobs of his life: chief mechanic on Sir Edmund Hillary's 1958 expedition to the South Pole.

'Ed Hillary's dad was a bee-keeper and he had one of my

honey extractors,' recalls Jim. 'Ed didn't know anything about
any of the other applicants for the engineer's job, but he knew
about my honey extractor — it even had my name on it. The other
applicants were recommended by the Army and the Navy, but Ed
— the son of a bee-keeper — insisted on me, the son of another
bee-keeper.'

So Uncle Jim had the job of keeping the Massey Ferguson
tractors running all the way to the South Pole. Good old workhorse
tractors from a typical Kiwi farm, and there they were with tank
tracks on the wheels and my Uncle Jim poking about beneath the
bonnets. Jim was responsible for keeping the things working and
he took all this equipment down to Antarctica where they set up
camp to prepare for the expedition. As soon as they arrived on the
ice, he built this bloody great big shed. Some of the guys in the
expedition were pissed off because they wanted to get cracking on
other things — like driving to the South Pole. Hillary was fuming.
But my Uncle Jim told Ed Hillary: 'You can't fix a tractor without a
shed!' There's Kiwi wisdom for you.

'And of course,' says Uncle Jim, 'Ed was one of the first to use
the shed.'

That expedition consolidated the image of Kiwis and our can-
do attitude: once we're on a mission we never give up and we
find solutions to seemingly insurmountable problems on the spot.
This is something I live by. I was always impressed by guys like
Jim, and inspired by them. They showed me you could do a hell
of a lot by using some gumption, a little know-how and, of course,
some number eight wire. You didn't need to have a bit of paper on
the wall if you could prove yourself in the field. These are broad
principles that have guided me in business to this day. They're
also the traits I've tended to look for in the people I have working

for and with me.

Fear of letting down my parents and family, especially my grandparents and uncles, kept me on the straight and narrow (mostly) as I was growing up. I was always too scared to do anything to piss them off or disappoint them. But I still had some great adventures along the way.

I had realised pretty early on that the mainstream education system wasn't going to do a hell of a lot for me, and I knew I wouldn't get much out of higher education. In fact, at fifteen the only thing that had me seriously thinking about going back to school for another year was the prospect of playing another season of rugby with my friends. This is where my mum stepped in.

'AJ, you can leave school at the end of the fifth form — once you've sat your school certificate — provided that you have a permanent job lined up. If not, you have to stay at school — I won't have you sitting about the house.'

So when a mate's father — Norm Sample from the North Shore Tramping Club, who was a foreman at a construction company — said that he could line me up a full-time job when I was still at school, I grabbed the opportunity. At sixteen, I was off to learn the building trade as an apprentice carpenter-joiner. I was out of school in December, hitched down to Queenstown with a mate for New Year's Eve and was into a builder's pinny by mid-January. It took three-and-a-half years to finish the 8000 hours for my apprenticeship. That's a lot of sweat, toil and bruised thumb nails, but I loved it.

The sense of satisfaction you get from building from scratch is fantastic. Today, I still get a great buzz from building things, whether it's knocking my farmhouse in the French Alps into shape or doing work on a bungy tower 40 metres in the air above the teeming masses of Bali. Whenever we've developed bungy sites — starting with the first one in Ohakune — I've been in there, hammering away.

There were two senior sergeants at Takapuna Police Station when I was in my teens. One was my neighbour Ray East, a good bloke, and the other was a guy called Ross Meurant, who went on to lead the Red Squad, the police riot unit during the anti-apartheid protests that came with the Springbok rugby tour of 1981. He later became a right-wing politician and ended up in parliament. When he worked the beat in my neighbourhood, Meurant was — in my opinion — a bully and an oaf. He picked on young blokes simply because he had the power to do so and he didn't like me because I had long hair, wore jeans and went to parties late at night.

He seemed to love watching people cringe. One morning while hitching home from a party, Meurant pulled up alongside me and hauled me off to the cells. Before chucking me in the cell for the night, I had to empty my pockets. When it came time for me to be released the following morning, some of the money I had checked in had gone. My hard-earned cash had disappeared while I was locked in a police station. Later, the Takapuna Police graciously sent me a receipt for the missing money (but not the cash itself), after my mum had kicked up merry hell.

This guy and his attitudes were a large part of me wanting to move away from Auckland. I have no problem with the majority of cops as individuals, but Meurant eroded a lot of my faith in the police force as a system. I know plenty of others who grew up on the Shore with me who now have reduced respect for the law, on account of dealing with the likes of Meurant, and these aren't bad people, they are typical law-abiding Kiwis, respectable and successful businessmen with families.

I was developing a great love of the outdoors and skiing in particular. I would get as much time down at Ruapehu as possible in the winter and in the summer I was out rock climbing, on trips with the North Shore Tramping Club, or away on lengthy surf trips with mates from the Shore.

We had some brilliant times on the surfing tours. We'd either drive or hitch to beaches all over the North Island. On one hitch-hiking trip with my mate Pete Demooij, the two of us were having a hard time getting back to Auckland. Fortunately, I had long hair (okay, a mullet) and — Pete tells me — a reasonably tidy butt. So he hid in the bushes on the side of the road and I sashayed along like a lone female hitch-hiker, my bag over my shoulder and my hair flowing. I'm flattered that we didn't have to wait long for a ride to arrive.

On another surfing trip, this time to Gisborne, we were really unimpressed with the food in this restaurant, so we did a runner. This was out of order but pretty low level in terms of police priorities. What wasn't so smart on our part was that two of the guys in our group had been in the same restaurant and done a runner the night before, so the manager was watching us and when we bolted he was out the door and on our tails in a flash.

But the dumbest thing was yet to come. Unbeknownst to us there had been a jewellery heist in town that day. Jewellery in Gisborne — go figure. One of the fellas in the group, a guy called Pete, had run the other way out of the restaurant and found himself being chased by half of the Gisborne police force. He thought it was strange that so many police were out for an unpaid restaurant bill, and eventually he hid under a bridge. He tucked in there, but a cop had him covered, thinking that he was the armed jewellery thief. The cop followed him under the bridge and burst out screaming 'freeze' and pointing his gun. And Pete's thinking: 'Shit fella, it was only a cheap steak.' They took him to the cop shop and while he was being processed, the cop left the room and he jumped out the window and ran over to the campsite where we were. He yells: 'Guys, we've gotta get outta here.'

The only problem being we had no money and hardly any gas for the car so we had to do a bottle run. In every town we went through on the way from Gisborne to Auckland we stopped and knocked on doors to ask if there were any glass bottles we could trade in at the recycling centre. It was a long ride home.

My adventures away from work were fun and the job was great too. As much as I loved the building gig, when my apprenticeship finished I was really keen for some new challenges — travel was beckoning. The last day of my apprenticeship was a Wednesday and on the Friday I drove down to Mt Hutt in the South Island to finish the ski season. Predictably, I ended up broke before long so I found myself working as a liftie for a bit to cover my costs. It was an interesting time as I saw more of the culture that goes with working on a ski-field and in the tourism industry; I felt at home in that environment. There were interesting people to meet — travellers on holiday and fellow workers who came from the four corners of the globe — and the atmosphere was always pretty friendly on and off the piste.

At the end of that season at Mt Hutt, an old mate called Peter

Sutherland and I decided we would have a go at opening a ski shop in Fairlie because there was a new ski-field opening there. Cash was a problem — we needed a big injection of it in a hurry — and I didn't fancy labouring on a building site in New Zealand for the amount of time it would take to make the sort of money we needed. Eventually, I figured there'd be good money in mining in Western Australia, so I flew out to Perth. But the money wasn't what I thought it would be and the work wasn't as plentiful, so I found myself casting around for something else to do. I was staying in a youth hostel and I was kicking myself for having travelled all that way just to be broke, when one day I saw an ad in the paper — 'Young interesting people wanted', 'loads of travel' and (crucially) 'top money'.

That's how I became an encyclopedia salesman. It was the first time I'd really taken on a job that involved figuring out people rather than figuring out practical things. Now, I was born with the gift of the gab — and I spent a lot of time polishing that gift as I grew up — but here was a chance to develop it and put it to good use. And by God, did I put it to good use.

It wasn't until after I had quit selling the books that the realisation of exactly what I had been doing hit me — walking into the homes of complete strangers and selling them a thousand dollars worth of books, and locking them really hard into the deal in the course of it. I learnt a lot about selling and dealing with people from that negotiating experience, but I found every time I was talking to people I was manipulating them, which is a core part of that kind of direct sales programme. I could put them wherever I wanted to put them. We had a set presentation we ran through to sell these books, but I found that I was so bloody good that I was sorting out people's objections and concerns before they even emerged. It started to freak me out how good I was at selling these encyclopedias; it made me feel uncomfortable, but the sales kept rolling in. I could look at a house and say: 'Yep, station wagon in the driveway, nicely mown lawn, nappies on the line, concerned about the kids' education, probably smoke a pack of cigarettes a day and send two kids off to the school down the road.'

It just felt horrible to be constantly sizing up people for the opportunity to exploit them. Welcome to the world of encyclopedia salesmanship, AJ Hackett. Shit, when it comes to it, welcome to the world of business. But the skills I learnt in that period — and the realisation that I could make such potent use of those skills — set me up for life.

I packed in the job in Perth after about four months to return to New Zealand and, as it turns out, I was the top encyclopedia salesman in Australasia. The encyclopedia guys were keen for me to continue selling for them back home, so I took it on with my own little crew of sales staff. We'd nip around the country flicking these things off. Eventually, I fell for a girl who was working in my team — Susie Pascoe became the first great love of my life and we quit the encyclopedia gig altogether to seek new adventures.

For the first time in my life, but not the last, I turned my back on a successful business situation to take on something new. It's not overstating things for me to say that I would have made a fortune if I had stayed in that sales sector. A few years later, I turned my back completely on the very successful building company that I had established in order to throw my energies into bungy jumping. To be really successful in business, and in life, you've got to be prepared to walk away from something — even if it is a successful enterprise — and throw yourself into something new. You've got to have the belief that you are smart enough and talented enough to make the next project work just as well as the last thing you did. You have to believe that the reason you succeeded once was because you're bloody good, not simply because of dumb luck. Only through that kind of self-belief will you find yourself doing what's truly right for you, instead of settling for second best because of fear of failure.

Susie and I built a house truck and spent four years cruising around New Zealand. We visited every part of the most beautiful country on earth, checking out new places and making friends every step of the way. I became great friends with Susie's parents, Alec and Judy, and her family became mine. Alec was a thoughtful and worldly man who introduced me to some of the finer things in life, like red wine, art and sensible conversation. So great was my respect for Susie's family that, years after we had split up, I named my eldest son Dean, after her brother who was a really cool dude.

After we tired of the nomadic life, Susie and I moved the house truck from Russell in the Bay of Islands, where we had a contract to build a house, and we parked it out the back of an old villa that we had bought in Auckland. I spent my days pottering around fixing up this villa in Mt Eden and taking on building work around the city. Gradually, my business built up until I was employing about half a dozen lads on construction jobs, specialising in one-off, difficult renovations that other firms wouldn't touch. Building permits were optional, which led us to many an interesting run-in with building inspectors. And that was about the point when I got the call from Chris Sigglekow.

CHAPTER 3

French
lessons

I arrived in Europe in February 1987 as a member of the
New Zealand speed skiing team — yep, that famous sporting
juggernaut, the Kiwi speed skiers. There were four of us and we
were all good keen Kiwi boys, willing to belt down a hill as hard
as we could. It's fair to say that selection in the squad for the winter
season in Europe depended more on your willingness to pay for
some really long skis, some tight trousers and an air ticket, and
your capacity to hurtle hungover down an icy slope, than on any
ability to actually look the Austrians in the eye when it came to
divvying up the prizes. But it was great fun.

Henry van Asch and Martin Jones, who had both come bungy
jumping with us in Hamilton, were genuinely very good at speed
skiing. Aided by a strong competitive streak, Henry had set a New
Zealand speed skiing record of 159.5 kph flying downhill at Turoa

in 1986, and he set another one on that tour when he hit 192.72 kph at Les Arcs in France, taking the record back from Martin Jones. In the two decades since we went on that tour, the speeds have increased frighteningly, so much so that Chris Gebbie's Kiwi record now stands at a jaw-dropping 232.86 kph and the world record is nudging a death-defying 250 kph.

I love to ski these days and the village in France I've settled down in is surrounded by some of the best ski fields and snow conditions in Europe. I'm a better skier now than I was then, but today I'm more interested in working my way around a field with my kids, exploring the mountain and encouraging them to extend their limits rather than spending my time chasing records.

The speed skiing we were involved in took place on specialised courses, which the competitors had to prepare. This involved marching up and down the hill in your ski boots, packing the snow in hard, and then side-stepping in skis until the track was immaculately groomed and incredibly slick. Racers would start with a mammoth drop — pretty much a sheer plummet — tucking into the most aerodynamic position possible before the slope flattened out and then holding your speed through a 100-metre timing trap — we were ranked according to the average speed for that 100 metres.

The social life was great. In fact, sometimes the social life impinged on our sporting endeavours. One morning I found myself launching down the slope on a freezing cold day in Sweden when suddenly I realised that the razor-cold wind was blasting straight into my eyes, and hurting like hell. Sure enough, I had been so nervous and wound up at the start of my run that I had left the visor on my helmet in a raised position. Effectively blinded while tucked into the maximum speed position and dropping down an almost 90-degree slope, all I could do as I plummeted at frightening speed was to veer off the track. That was pretty much the end of speed skiing for me.

The tour was fantastic. I developed a love of European culture and society that has stayed with me ever since, prompting me to settle on the continent and live in France for two decades. I married a Frenchwoman, Caroline, and we went on to raise three beautiful children in France — Dean, Jayde and Margaux. In my time I've found a real affinity between Kiwis and the French: the French have this exciting, rather debonair, streak about them and Kiwis are up for pretty much anything. There's a love of life, adventure and sensation that makes the two national characteristics rather similar, so there's a strong sense of kindred spirit and mutual respect between the two cultures. As the bungy jumping got bigger around the world and the AJ Hackett brand got huge in New Zealand, I came to be incredibly grateful for the relative peace of a quiet spot in France. The respite of living in a French community where I could simply be AJ, whose kids go to the local school and who runs a little business from home, was much more manageable than being AJ Hackett, the adventure tourism icon in New Zealand.

In my first European winter, we eventually reached the French Alps where we settled in for the finish of the ski season. Chris Sigglekow had compiled a tape of all the jumps that he and I had done back in New Zealand, and I had taken to impressing locals and fellow skiers — or at least trying to impress them — with tales of our bungy exploits. When we were at a bar in La Clusaz, in

France, I played this VHS cassette and was standing about telling people about what we did when a guy approached me with a steely look in his eye. He grasped my hand and said: 'You must jump the Pont de la Caille.'

'Huh?'

'You must jump the Pont de la Caille! It will be great for you and your rubber bands!'

I finally realised that he was talking about a bridge that I could bungy off.

There were actually two bridges spanning a beautiful gorge. One was an old abandoned suspension bridge — 147 metres high — which no one ever used, making it ideal for bungy jumping. It was perfect; a real ripper of a viaduct stretching over a mighty valley, with a river below. I had hoped to find something to jump off while on this tour and I could not have asked for anything better than the Pont de la Caille.

Within a couple of weeks of being in France, I was back into the bungy buzz! We sussed out a place in Lyon where we could get rubber and some chemists who were working there helped me out and gave me a lot of advice. It was the first time that I had really learned heaps about the actual material we were using and relying on for the preservation of our lives. With the help of those chemists, I found out a lot more about what rubber could do and how it worked.

One of the things I had been wondering about was what would happen if I used the rubber in extremely cold conditions. I had a fantasy about bungy jumping out of a cable car above a ski field and then skiing down it. There was a ski field nearby at Tignes which had already caught my eye.

First I had to get the ball rolling by performing the first-ever bungy jump on the continent. I rounded up some gear — ropes, karabiners and other climbing equipment — from local outdoor equipment suppliers and put the actual bungy together from the strands of rubber I'd bought. I joined up with Martin Jones, who had bungied with me before, and a couple of local boys from a bar we had been drinking in right next to the bridge. We headed over to the bridge and I rigged up the necessary gear. It was freezing cold, so the consumption of a couple of mulled wines was critical before the French guys started on the 5-kilometre drive down to the valley where they were going to help get me out of the bungy cord after I had completed my jump. I showed Martin how to lower me once the bungy had finished twanging and told him to drive down to the bottom of the gorge to pick me up when everything was sorted up top. It was a fair old way down there.

With everything rigged up, I climbed over the barrier. For the first jump in France I planned a head-first dive, with an ankle tie. It was to be the highest jump I'd done up to that time with this type of harness. I'd previously jumped with an ankle tie from the Auckland Harbour Bridge but that was only about 40 metres. This time the jump was about 130 metres — a big bastard. There was some debate as to what would happen to me as the blood rushed to my head. Would I black out?

I waved to our French mates — who spoke no English at all — just as the sun was starting to set, then I shuffled along so that my toes were edging out into space. Martin joined me in the countdown and I launched outwards into what was to become the classic arms-out, swallow dive. And what a flight! No worries about blacking out here — this was easily the best jump I had ever done. I howled with glee as I dropped into the gorgeous isolated valley in the fading twilight sun. Bouncing up, I yelled to Martin about what a great jump it was and called out to the two French guys down the bottom. Eventually, the cord settled and Martin began to lower me, just as I had shown him.

I was trussed up by the ankles and needed someone to help undo the ties that bound me so that I could clamber down. Martin lowered me a little further towards the cold water below. And further still. Er, hang on mate! With one last sudden drop, he lowered me straight into the freezing Alpine river. I was waist deep, and upside down, in the coldest water imaginable. Shocked, I curled up out of the water and howled to Martin to raise me a little so I wouldn't drown or freeze. I then called over to the French lads to get them to wade in. Martin couldn't hear as he was already on his way to the car to drive down and pick me up. After the 5-kilometre drive, he had a kilometre jog to get to where he was to help me down.

The French guys wouldn't come into the water to pull me out — I figured the water must have been pretty deep with a strong current — even though I was only six metres away from them. The pair of them were leaning out to me with sticks in a bid to hook me in. So I'm dangling by my feet with the choice of either hanging with my torso submerged in freezing water or attempting some sort of pained half-sit-up position while I waited for Martin to come and figure out how to get me down. It was the end of February, so it was as cold as hell, with ice everywhere, the sun had gone from the gorge by this point and there was plenty of snow on the surrounding mountains. The water was beyond cold and getting colder. I was cursing at the French guys to come and help me out, but they spoke no English and I spoke no French. I suspect they were a bit useless anyway, dangling their sticks at me, always just out of my reach. I was thinking the French guys couldn't have been very good swimmers or something — surely they'd come to pull me out otherwise?

Eventually, my whole body was tiring and to get a moment's release from my painful position, I unfurled my torso so my head was briefly submerged in the water. I let my arms stretch down. Hello, what was this? It was the riverbed. The bloody river was only a couple of feet deep. The French guys were solely worried about keeping their shoes and trousers dry! Holding my breath and clawing my way along the bottom of the river bed, like a trussed turkey in a bid for freedom, I edged my way out of the water just as Martin arrived on the scene to pull me out. As we all retired back to the bar near the bridge to warm up and celebrate, I made a mental note to learn some good French swear words.

Despite my refrigerated dip, the jump had been a great success, so after that little session we started going down to that bridge a lot. The boys on the New Zealand speed skiing team, and a couple of French mates, Denys Porte and his friend Albert, became the nucleus of the bungy industry. Henry and I went on to launch and run the biggest bungy company in the world. Chris Allum, who travelled with the speed skiing team the following year, worked with us in Ohakune and Queenstown and eventually set up an operation of his own in New York. Denys also operated all over Europe and the US, developing many new concepts in bungy.

I was determined to jump from a gondola. There was a cracking opportunity to jump at Tignes where a gondola gave me a good 91-metre drop into snow below. It was part of my dream of bungying down, undoing the cord and skiing away. But for starters it seemed smart to simply get the bungy jump sorted out first. The owners of the ski field were happy to have me jump there, provided that I did it when the area was not in use, which meant either first thing in the morning or last thing at the end of the day. Either way, it would be freezing cold. We opted for first thing in the morning, with crisp early sun making for some dramatic footage for both film and stills photography. I planned to use this jump as a way of selling the bungy concept to people as a promotional exercise, so good footage was crucial. We also wanted to see what effect the extreme cold would have on the rubber.

And I mean very extreme cold. The temperature standing at the door of the gondola moments before throwing myself out was −15 degrees without wind chill. Anyone who touched a metal surface with exposed skin, stuck to it. When I flew out the door, the cold air struck my cheek like sharp nettles, but the drop was wonderful — a bungy over a snowfield makes for spectacular viewing. I had hoped to get a little powder touch at the bottom but realised as the surface rushed up towards me that I was going down way too fast. We had a little too much bungy cord. Impact was imminent and, despite the snow, I knew the surface would be hard. I had been learning karate, so I reflexively tucked my head out of the way and hammered the snow with two good strong fists, making it possible for the rest of my body to plough in. I went into the snow as far as my waist before the bungy cord ripped me out again. A great jump, a bit of a close call, but no harm done. And the footage was fantastic.

Skiing in the Haute-Savoie region was brilliant, and when we weren't up the mountain a few of us would head down to the Pont de la Caille for a bungy session. Mostly it was me and a few

French pals, but a few of the Kiwi boys also came along. By the end of the winter, we'd had such a great time that we decided to throw a big party down at the bridge for a bunch of our mates so that we could thank everyone who'd been so cool to us all that season. The idea was that we could have people jumping who hadn't jumped before, and everyone would have a few drinks and hang out for a bit watching the action on the bridge and seeing how we had been spending our time. A close friend, Didi Hasse, had a clothing company called Tapis Volant, which we named the party after. He later supplied a shop with clothing which I set up in Ohakune.

On the morning of the party, Henry did a very special jump — probably as radical as any jump I've ever seen to this day. Jaque Gris, a friend who worked locally for Look, the French cycling company, offered Henry a bike if he would jump with it. It was a novel idea, and it certainly caught Henry's attention. We stretched the bungy between two bridges to create a catapault system in order to launch Henry out into space on the mountain bike. Henry was hooked to the bike, the bike was connected to the next bridge by a bungy cord which we cranked up as tight as we could and both Henry and the bike were held in place for take-off by some strong webbing. I took a knife and cut the webbing holding Henry in place and — boom — he just flew. I've never seen anything like it. Henry was stoked, and the bike he got for doing it was just reward for having sizeable cojones.

Setting up that launch was a major operation — it took most of the morning. Then in the afternoon our mates started arriving. Then more of them arrived. And even more mates, along with a few strangers, followed. Pretty soon it was manic, with a fantastic party atmosphere as people gathered around bonfires down in

Mum playing snakes and ladders in Australia, 1956.

Mum at Fox Glacier in the early 1950s.

The original members
of the Trolley Brigade:
top row, Colin Louden,
Robin Louden, Gordon
Thomas, Robbie
Thomas, Elaine,
me; front row: Steve
Thomas, Kitty, Anna,
Bryce Reagan.

LEFT: North Shore
Tramping Club week
at Mount Egmont.
Mum, me, Anna and
Elaine.

My last year at school. I'm in the back row, fourth from the left.

Vine jumping,
Pentecost Island,
Vanuatu.

Chris Sigglekow jumping from Pelorus Bridge, 1980.

Chris releasing himself from the parachute harness, Pelorus Bridge, 1980.

The two Susies, our first female jumpers and great friends, Auckland 1986.

First jump, Hamilton, 1986.

Our housetruck — home for almost five years.

ABOVE: Henry van Asch and I mono-skiing (and getting disqualified in the process!) in the Powder 8s competition in Wanaka, 1987.

LEFT: Mark, Chris and I before the first big jump — Rangitikei Viaduct, central North Island.

ABOVE: *Chris and I jumping from Auckland Harbour Bridge while the police launch, Deodar, watches on.*

RIGHT: *Me relaxing on the back of the Deodar, while Chris gets out of his harness.*

ABOVE: *Practising for the Eiffel Tower jump, me executing a classic dive from Pont de la Caille, France, 1987.*

RIGHT: One of the close calls — a bungy tangle at the Pont de la Caille, France, 1987.

the valley and jumpers lined up on the bridge. Within a couple of hours we had about 200 people there, the music was pumping and everyone was gagging to do a bungy. Booze was flowing. People who were driving past would just pull over to see what was going on and then join in the party. We had two bungy systems going, one on either side of the bridge, so we were jumping people constantly. As Jaque Gris jumped, he yelled: 'It's only rock and roll!'

'I like it!' I called back.

Ropes, bungy cords and karabiners were lying all over the place and the crowds of people down in the valley who were gathered outside an old abandoned casino by the river would let out great roars of encouragement every time someone stepped out to the edge to make their jump. Excitable French friends were tearing about the place yelling: 'I want to do a jump now AJ!' 'Non! Me next!'

The party was great and everyone was having a blast, running around like wide-eyed kids at a candy party, but on the bridge it was mayhem and we were rapidly losing track of what was going on.

And that was when we nearly killed a good mate. My Swiss friend Dominic had the bungy around his feet and was over the handrail ready to go. 'I'm ready now! Shall I jump AJ?'

He was leaning out, slowly tipping forward with his arms rising into the crucifix position. Dominic was about half a second away from a one-way plunge. I was a bit flustered and hadn't even realised he was out there ready to go. 'Um, hang on, mate . . .' Had someone else prepared him for the jump? I looked around and saw that the other end of the bungy cord wasn't even hooked to anything. He was going to die. 'Stop!' I yelled, lunging for the guy.

'Stop! Shit — hold on mate! Hold on!' I grabbed him just in time and when he saw the unattached end of the bungy cord in my hand, Dominic quickly clutched towards me for help and a couple of us hauled him back in. That was a very sobering experience.

After managing about 20 jumps, I went over the side myself to join in the party down below, leaving Henry and Denys in charge. An hour later Henry radioed to tell me that things on the bridge were too manic and he wanted to wrap it up. It was too chaotic; he was getting flustered. To make matters worse, someone had stolen his brand-new, shiny Look bicycle. So we had to stop at that point.

Henry and I sat down later and we figured that there were two or three near-death situations up on the bridge which we had narrowly avoided in that little session. This was the first time I had ever been responsible for a large-scale, public jumping exercise and the consequences had nearly been disastrous. Clearly I needed to make sure I always had control of the situation if other people were around on a bungy site. It taught us something about the importance of safety and taking things one logical step at a time at our own speed, especially when we were jumping other people. People who were new to it would never be as cool-headed as we were. It was all well and good when we were the ones on the end of the bungy cord, because we were highly unlikely to go over the side without making sure everything was sorted. But there was an element of mass hysteria that made everything go a bit leery on the bridge that evening.

And that was the other thing that the party session on the Pont de la Caille and the atmosphere in the valley below taught me about: mass hysteria. This crowd had absolutely loved bungy jumping. Not just doing it, but actually being there while it was being done. People were having a great time hanging out and watching this cool new activity take place. They were transfixed by the sight of other people falling and bouncing about on the end of a rubber band. When the jumper got off at the bottom they brought a phenomenal energy with them that vitalised the crowd. That meant bungy jumping had to have some sort of commercial potential. The encyclopedia salesman deep inside me saw an opportunity.

The rest of the Kiwi ski team had already gone back to New Zealand and Henry was the last to leave. I stayed on for another six weeks — there was a certain tower in Paris I wanted to jump off.

It was never my intention to offer paying members of the public the chance to have a go at bungy jumping for themselves. I had no interest in that at all; bungy was far too personal a thing for me — it was a friends-only gig. The experience of that party at Pont de la Caille had shocked me somewhat. My first idea for a business model was based around the idea of large one-off event jumps — with me doing a big leap to launch some product or to publicise some sort of marketing campaign. Looking back now, I see that I was naive to think that I could limit or control the commercial growth of this thing. Or that I could hold back people's desire to be the ones doing the jumping. But the idea of building and managing permanent sites where people would pay good cash to jump themselves was a big step away from what I was considering.

What terrified me the most about having other people pay to jump was the thought that we could kill someone. Safe bungy jumping meant cutting down on the variables — if we all knew our shit, then nothing could go wrong. The problem was that at the time I was the only jump-master, and everyone else still had a lot to learn. The experience at Pont de la Caille had shown me that introducing new people to jumping meant that we were introducing new variables. Every person reacted differently to standing on the edge of a platform way above the ground and every person reacted differently to having the cord attached to them. Safe jumping would clearly require a lot of specialised knowledge. I liked the idea of one jumper with a tight team around him, sorting out things and making sure that every single aspect of the jump was perfect.

When I left the mountains for Paris, I did a swap with my friends Denys and Albert: they took two of the bungy cords we'd been using at Pont de la Caille and in return they gave me a parapente. I liked the idea of trying out parapenting; and those two liked doing anything crazy. They had been jumping with us and helping out all winter, so I taught them how to use the bungy safely, and that pretty much planted the seeds of the European bungy industry. All of our friends in France were pretty radical; they were climbers, extreme skiers and hang-glider pilots, or they were into flying off things and parachuting. I guess it was natural that they would take the bungy we started and do surprising things with it.

In years to come, Denys travelled all over the continent putting on bungy demonstrations and setting up for paid jumpers. He also tried out some new and unconventional tricks with the bungy — one favourite was to hook up the cord at the top of a sheer cliff face and run down the cliff, smashing through trees and obstacles until the cord pulled taut and twanged him back, dragging him along the cliff. Not advisable. The evolution of bungy in France was mind-blowing. Whereas we had started out on small bridges, doing things cautiously, the guys who started out with us on the Pont de la Caille just went haywire from there. They used the cords I gave them to set up a catapault for speed skiing — it was radical acceleration from zero to nearly 160 kph in an instant. Absolutely insane stuff. It was also a fair indication of how excitable the French can be when they have an adrenalin sport and some spare time on their hands.

Six weeks after the party on Pont de la Caille, I jumped off the Eiffel Tower. From that point on, the whole bungy phenomenon took on a life of its own and it didn't matter how I thought the thing should be developed — pretty soon everyone wanted to do one for themselves. The ball was rolling.

CHAPTER 4

A bloody
great leap
of faith

On a warm June night in 1987, I stood beneath the Eiffel Tower. If you've ever seen the tower at night, you'll know why the French are so proud of it. On a clear night like this one, the array of lights spread all over the structure look stunning. Day or night, the tower commands attention from all over Paris. But on this night I wasn't taking in its beauty. I was on a mission.

The next morning at sunrise, on 26 June, I was going to bungy jump from the second level of the Eiffel Tower, 110 metres above the ground. With pre-arranged camera crews in strategic positions ready to beam the images around the world, this jump would launch bungy to the planet. It was no longer going to be just me and some mates jumping off things in the south of France or out the back end of Ohakune. This would be huge. Looking back now, there's no doubt that this jump marked the real beginning of the bungy phenomenon. From the moment I threw myself over the side of the Eiffel Tower, bungy grew and grew, taking on a life of its own along the way.

First things first though, we had to get a bungy team and camera crew hidden away on the tower overnight, tucked into sleeping bags in the chilly rafters, so the jump could go ahead at first light. As far as checking to see if I was allowed to jump, I operated on the premise that it's better to ask forgiveness than to seek permission. This was to be top secret stuff. I had done my homework, casing the joint thoroughly from below and within. For more than a month beforehand I'd visited the tower regularly, checking on what the guards did, and when they did it.

I went up to the various levels regularly and found out where the cameras were and what points on and around the tower attracted relatively less attention from the security team. I found out what time the first guards arrived in the morning and when the last ones left at night. Bungy jumping wasn't illegal — it wasn't even heard of — but there was little doubt that if the Eiffel Tower's management, or the local gendarmerie, found out what we were up to, they would come down on us like a tonne of bricks and the jump would be cancelled. Secrecy was essential. Weeks in advance, from a stake-out position beneath the tower, I formatted a complicated table showing when the lights on the various platforms were switched on and off. I sat surrounded by people with sketchpads — they were drawing the tower and I was drawing up my scheme.

We found the best exits in case the whole thing went belly-up and a quick getaway was called for. On the tower itself, we tested the distractability of the guards: how long could you keep one of them from making routine checks when armed with nothing more than some daft questions and a bit of pleasant conversation? It's fair to say that for one month in 1987, I knew more about the security of the Eiffel Tower than the people who were actually charged with securing this beauty. It's also fair to say that the security got a substantial shake-up once we had finished our business up there.

Crucially, I had done the fishing-line test; dropping a small piece of nylon line with a weight on the end to get the exact distance from the point that I would jump from. You can always find books or blueprints of structures that will tell you how tall something is, and architect's drawings that will show you possible obstacles to a big jump, but nothing beats the peace of mind of standing there and lowering a humble strand of fishing line. With all due respect to the architects and draughtsmen, I like to verify measurements myself — especially when it's my balls that are on the line.

I managed to do the fishing line measuring test about a month or so before the jump itself. It was on one of my first reconnaissance visits up the tower and I was taking in a lot of the security procedures, watching out for dozy Frenchmen sidling around the place in uniform. On a crisp morning, I quickly glanced over my shoulders to check for security, and then chucked the line over. I turned my back to the barrier and leaned against it, adopting a nonchalant look — well as close to a nonchalant look as you can adopt when dangling a nylon line off the Eiffel Tower. I had a pre-rehearsed alibi at the ready: 'I'm just fishing, mate!' — which I figured would probably see me thrown out of the place as a nutter, but not locked up as a criminal. Other than some understandably odd glances from a couple of passing tourists, there was no interference.

It gave me a sense of reassurance, holding my end of that fishing line, while a mate below touched his end to the ground so we could mark off the distance. In a way, it's the first step to conquering the space between the point you're jumping from and the ground. Standing there, 110 metres above the ground, I could visualise myself jumping, the cord unravelling behind me, arms outstretched — triumphant.

Once we had measured the distance, my mate Kelly Sori and I travelled down to the Pont de la Caille. We did about 20 jumps off the thing, just getting the system down pat. We tested again and again, with Sori lowering me so he was really comfortable with the whole procedure. He was a sound jump operator with a good head on his shoulders and that gave me a lot of confidence about the whole jump.

I'd made a deal with a big production house called Sygma, and it was important that they were comfortable with filming the whole thing too, so we got them to come along to see what was going on and to figure out what they would need to make it work visually. There would be only one chance to capture these images. Our deal was simple: basically, I covered the cost of the bungy and Sygma covered the (somewhat more substantial) cost of shooting the jump with video and still photography. We were to split the profits made from selling the footage and photographs worldwide. I figured there could be good money in it — and in the end my cut of the profit covered most of my winter expenses, manna from heaven for a ski bum.

The main thing for me was that I wanted to open up other commercial possibilities for taking bungy into promotional and marketing work. When the stunning visuals of the jump went worldwide, I was confident that I could move on to more big jumps and turn this hobby of mine into a fun lifestyle with a serious income.

The night before the jump, about an hour before closing time on the tower, my team gathered beneath the massive structure. One by one, we emerged from the darkness, each arriving from a different direction and each carrying items crucial for the operation — rope, bungy cord, karabiners, bits of webbing, the camera gear and the harness. And, of course, sleeping bags — we were going to be sleeping rough up on the national symbol of France. It was late at night — past 10 pm and nearing closing time for the viewing platforms on the tower — and once we had gathered at ground level, our cunning plan called for everyone to meet at one spot up on the structure.

There were about a dozen of us in total; we paid our entry fees and went in separately, so as not to attract too much attention — I figured that a lift packed full of people carrying large bags just before closing time would attract the attention of even the dopiest guards. One by one we trickled in and made our way to the meeting point — a bar on the level I was jumping from. My mouth was pretty dry at this point; I was hellishly nervous about someone in the group being stopped and searched on their way up. But everyone made it in, so I enjoyed a beer and a moment to catch my breath. Looking around the faces of the team, I saw a mixture of nervousness and excitement — we were enthusiastic amateurs playing at some sort of warped espionage game.

We even synchronised our watches, which sounds a tad excessive in hindsight, but timing was crucial to the exercise.

We wished each other good luck and then I sent the team off to their predetermined points. The core of the squad was to climb over a fence and into a wee maintenance annex that was off-limits to the public — it was there we would set up camp for the night, out of sight of the guards. The rest were busy running interference with guards and blocking select security cameras with umbrellas and bits of cardboard as we scaled the fence.

First we sent the girls downstairs — Caroline, my girlfriend at the time and future wife, and Shara, Sori's girlfriend, had a crucial role. Speaking frankly they're a pair of absolute stunners; and their mission was to play the role of eye candy at the exact moment that we were to climb the fence. They went downstairs to the room with the television monitors, where they had to occupy the guards' attention with their feminine wiles for ten minutes — a piece of cake for a pair of good-looking Frenchwomen.

The others dispersed to their pre-determined spots, each well drilled in what was required of them. Eventually only the core team was left — the overnighters. We made our way out of the bar and headed to the small stairwell that led to the fence we would climb. The place was clearing out by now, the few visitors left on the viewing platforms were making their way to the exits. I was feeling confident. Early on in the piece I figured we were most likely to be busted either by someone blabbing in the weeks leading up to the event, or when we gathered at the tower and made our way to the platform. Now we were dispersed in small groups, everything seemed straightforward; we just had to focus and stay calm. A chill was setting in for the night. I glanced around the overnight team as we made our way along the platform — Sori looked determined, and I knew I could count on him; one or two of the camera guys from Sygma seemed a bit excitable and edgy. We were getting close now. All I could think was, keep a cool head, AJ, and she'll be right, mate.

As we neared the spot where we had to leap the fence, I saw one or two of our camera blockers doing their jobs — they looked a bit odd to me standing around with umbrellas and sheets of cardboard in awkward poses, but no one else seemed to notice them. Other teams were hanging around in stairwells to obstruct people's passage through and gently detour them elsewhere. All the while, there was the very real risk that a security guard would walk by on a random check — the stairwell blockers were ready to keep guards busy with a series of daft questions. We walked on and suddenly we were at the fence leading to the annex, which was a couple of metres tall — my heart was racing now.

This was the bit where I guessed we were beginning to run foul of the law — a nice wee bit of trespass. I checked my watch and knew that right at that moment the girls were working their charm — that meant we had ten minutes to get into place. I glanced around, then sent the blokes over in waves, one or two at a time, passing the heavy gear over to them once they were on the other side of the fence. They each dashed to cover and made their way to a stairwell that led up under the floor above. There they had to leap a gate; it would have been easier to cut the padlock, but it was important to us that nothing was damaged on the tower. After a couple of waves had gone through, we got word that a security guard was coming by. We played it cool and spread out as if we were making our way to the exit like a regular bunch of tourists. The guard passed. Next wave — off you go boys. And you know what, we were such stars of the amateur espionage game that we did the whole manoeuvre in about four minutes.

There aren't many warm places to sleep 100-odd metres up in

the air on the Eiffel Tower, but we all set about finding the comfiest spots possible. I was feeling pretty bloody pleased with myself by now; the parts of the operation that seemed the riskiest in terms of getting caught had passed without major incident. I knew that the camera blockers and the girls were by now making their way downstairs and out of the structure. I'm patting myself on the back and setting up my sleeping bag, when I hear some loud voices. It's Sori, and in a flash he's pretty much having a shouting match with one of the camera crew. This isn't part of the plan. He can be pretty strong willed, old Kelly Sori. So, as I'm ducking out of sight and looking over to the public areas for any sign of the security guards, I'm hissing over to these stupid bastards to quit their shouting.

'What's going on? What the bloody hell are you doing, Sori?'

I knew about half a dozen words in French, but it was pretty clear that the ones these two fellas were exchanging weren't the kind you learn in a regular grammar class. As they snapped and snarled away at each other, their voices were rising even higher. I was peering about, terrified they were going to blow our cover. If a guard walked past at that point, we'd had it. I didn't want to expose myself by dashing over to where the two of them were arguing, but if the pair of them kept going on, they were sure to attract attention. I did that odd thing of trying to be heard above their noise while still speaking quietly — the best I could manage was a plaintive little, 'Fellas . . . what the hell's going on?!' Eventually Sori took a break from the Gallic shouting match and hissed to me that the bloody cameraman had lost his nerve and wanted to go home.

'You're joking.' We'd just smuggled ourselves, along with thousands of dollars worth of equipment, up the bloody Eiffel Tower to pull off a never-before-seen stunt, and the bloody cameraman wanted to go home!

But it was no joke. It turns out this cameraman had just got back from doing some filming work in the Middle East and his nerves were shot. He'd been back a couple of days after ducking bullets and seeing God knows what on the West Bank, and his bosses kindly send him to sleep the night on the Eiffel Tower with a couple of bungy nutters. He was pretty much shell-shocked and this clearly wasn't the ideal way to recover. He just couldn't handle the pressure, so he started arguing with Sori about going back down. As much as the whole thing irritated the hell out of me, I could see that there was nothing we could do about it. I was feeling kind of sorry for the guy. Sori by now had his hackles up, and was keen to force the poor bastard to stay. But I talked — or rather hissed — some sense into him and we helped the cameraman back over the fence.

Of course, at this point the girls were gone, the camera blockers were gone and our team had cleared the area. So all our best-laid plans were up in the air as the homesick cameraman scaled the fence and scarpered for the exit. I could see he was in a bad way and I just hoped that he could stay cool enough to avoid attention and not dob us in if he did get busted. We had a nervous half-hour wait until we were sure he was clear. It was a hiccup, but not a disaster — we still had two stills photographers up the tower with us and cameramen shooting from various points on the ground. Looking back, it would have been nice to have footage of the jump as we pieced it together from on top of the tower the next morning but, at the time, we simply put it behind us and got on with the task at hand — which, for now, involved settling into our sleeping bags and getting some shut eye.

Naturally, the next morning I slept in. Yep, on the biggest morning of my life — a dawn bungy jump off the Eiffel bloody Tower and the birth of the AJ Hackett Bungy empire — and what does AJ Hackett do? He gets an extra 30 minutes sleep. We had the jump arranged for first thing in the morning, when there would be the best light, and when there wouldn't be so many people around. With not a little swearing under my breath, I roused the lads and we got busy, clearing out of our sleeping annex and making our way to the jump point. It was still pretty dark but we all moved fast. Sori and I sorted out the fishing line for a test measure, running the line down for final confirmation of the height, as the photographers got into position.

Gradually we heard a noise coming from somewhere in the half light of pre-dawn. It was a steady clang, clang — it sounded like footsteps coming up the stairwell right next to us. Surely not! I had scoped all the security details and there were no guards due on the tower for at least an hour or so. Besides, who the hell would want to walk up the Eiffel Tower at such a painfully early hour of the morning? It was barely light and the security guys only started work when the lifts were operating. I feared the worst: someone must have shopped us, told the cops. Maybe the nervous cameraman had told someone. As the clanging grew louder, we ducked behind nearby walls and fixtures; teeth gritted, sweating and expecting to be busted. Then we heard voices, muttering in the gloom. Peeking incredulously around the wall, we watched as staff from the café above trudged past us on their way to work for the day. It was about a 30-storey hike to where we were and these guys went on up even further. Next time you think your daily

commute to work is rough, spare a thought for the kitchen hand
who has to walk up the Eiffel Tower every morning.

It was a pretty surreal moment. We looked at one another until
the noise from the café staff had passed — the guys were shaking
their heads and laughing inside — and then we went back to
getting ready for the jump. It was while I was leaning over the
barrier securing a line that I noticed a little pack of people on the
ground below, curled up peacefully asleep. There were a dozen or
so backpackers camping under the Eiffel Tower. I hadn't banked
on this. The first thing the guys on the ground had to do was clear
out those sleepers. Once woken, the backpackers naturally stood
around to watch the jump, and other people on their way to work
saw the backpackers and figured something was going on. Hey
presto: an instant crowd. The presence of the camera crew got the
gendarmes' attention — there are always a couple of them around
the base of the tower — and a few more of them appeared as
well. From high up on the platform I could see all this developing
below, but there was no turning back. There was only one way
down for me.

I figured we'd probably been seen, so Sori and I moved
through the final stages of the check pretty quickly. Dressed in a
tuxedo, with my feet strapped in and thumbs up signals all round,
I clambered over the fence. Sori was saying something, but I
blocked him out and took in the moment, champagne in hand.
We'd done the hard work, and this was what it was all about
— a bloke on the end of a cord leaping into space. And I did.
One small step for a man, a bloody great leap for the adventure
tourism industry. No one else had seen the Eiffel Tower from that
perspective — the ground rushing up and the four great struts
disappearing out the side of your vision — and lived to tell the

tale. It's a hell of a beautiful sight, I can tell you. When the cord hit and I twanged back up, suddenly it was like I was dancing in space between the grand arches of this magnificent tower.

Once they saw me jump, the cops all poured into the middle of the space below the tower. As I'm bouncing away, I can see them gathering below; one was waving me down, like he was directing traffic or something. When I bounced from one side to the other, the gendarmes all moved the same way with me — bonjour, Inspector Clouseau!

At this point I was meant to be spraying champagne over everyone — I had planned to grab a bottle from my friend Sophie Jeandel as the bungy reached its full extension, pop the cork and glug away in my tuxedo. Unfortunately, earlier on when we were setting up the rigging, I had misunderstood someone's call and had lifted the line up by about two metres, meaning I was about four metres clear of Sophie and the bubbly when the bungy fully extended. It would have made a nice image. On account of me mixing up this call, I was a good two metres too high to reach the damn bottle. It was a tricky measurement to get the champagne but it was a good thing that I didn't get it wrong two metres the other way — AJ Hackett with a faceful of dirt wouldn't have been the ideal image to sell bungy jumping to the world.

Once the bungy settled, Sori lowered me, and when I got to the ground Sophie and I swigged from the champagne bottle to toast a job well done — she had been instrumental in organising things for the jump. The press and police were running over to us, and I managed a quick interview for the cameras, standing there in my tux, bottle in hand, as the cops gathered in the background. 'AJ, what do you think the police will do?' asked the interviewer.

'I think they're reasonable people and I think they'll see it as an inspiration for the people of Paris, France and the world.'

In decades to come this prediction would prove very true.

I was still hooked by the ankles, and I had to tell all the police to stand back a bit as the rest of the bungy cord was about to come down behind me. The cops scattered just as the cord fell down, followed by the lowering rope, which hit the ground hard. Then, as the cameras rolled, they whisked me off to a nearby paddy wagon. As they were packing me into the back of the wagon, I saw Sori and the remaining guys from up the tower making their way down the stairs, totally unnoticed by the cops. They even gave me a cheerful wave! The gendarmes didn't know what the hell to do with me, so we made it easier for them: Sophie had my passport and a plane ticket, showing that I was about to clear out of the country. The cops looked at each other, still obviously not knowing what the hell was going on and what laws, if any, I may have broken. After some agitated discussion among themselves, they shoved me out of the police van and told me to clear off. Good lads.

We were blessed that day. Fortune favours the brave — nobody noticed us taking our place on the tower, the cameraman got out of there without being sighted and the café staff had not seen a thing. But our best bit of luck was that pretty much nothing else happened anywhere in the world that day. All of a sudden, bungy was beaming out on television news broadcasts globally and splattered all over the front pages of newspapers around the world. No major bombings, no major shootings. Just AJ Hackett, upside down in a tux.

The footage? Awesome. It made us all a handy bit of cash and had just the springboard effect for bungy jumping that I was after. There are great shots of the jump taken from the Trocadero, across the Seine. Although the people running the tower weren't too pleased with us at the time, today the jump is considered a vibrant part of the tower's history.

Over on the other side of the world, my sister Elaine got a call at her home in Sydney from Mum back in Auckland.

'Do you know what your brother has gone and done now?'

'It must be something daft or you would be calling him your son, not my brother.'

'He's gone and jumped off the Eiffel Tower and I've got all these reporters around the house. I can't leave the front door.'

Mum's been getting used to me jumping off stuff ever since.

CHAPTER 5

Balaclavas,
a crossbow and a canoe

With the success of the Eiffel Tower jump — both in terms of the mechanics of it and the publicity created by it — we had an opportunity to push this concept even further, taking bungy to a bigger audience. I hooked up with another production company wanting to film something spectacular. I had a mental image of a dawn bungy from the upraised arm of New York's Statue of Liberty. Filmed from a helicopter, we figured it would make for stunning visuals as I plummeted from the torch, which is 100 metres from the ground. Of course, it would also introduce bungy to the wealthy US market.

Organising the Eiffel Tower jump took a fair bit of Kiwi ingenuity, but it quickly became apparent that launching a jump from the Statue of Liberty would require just as much military precision. I devised an elaborate plan involving balaclavas, a crossbow and a canoe. Most of the operation was to take place in the dead of night. The idea was that I would make my jump just as the sun was rising. A camera crew on the ground and another airborne in a helicopter would film the whole thing. In terms of visuals, I thought it had the potential to be better than the Eiffel Tower leap; and there was that lucrative US market to think of. Next step: count the money from sales of the footage and sit back as the business deals for promotional jumps rolled in.

For the jump itself, I would have two of my mates from the ski tour with me, Chris Allum and Henry van Asch. So how did we end up locked in a police station cell? Where did it all go wrong?

The French production company sent a small crew ahead to line up all the materials we would need and sort out some of the logistics. But these French guys were useless, so when we got there five days before the jump, most of the gear we needed was still missing. The only thing these amateurs had managed to get us was a set of walkie-talkies that only worked when they were directly in line with each other. They also arranged accommodation for us in an apartment with a local artist who was undergoing a major cocaine-induced paranoia attack. After a few days of reassuring him that we weren't cops, we all moved to the Chelsea Hotel. Chris spent most of his time racing around trying to find a canoe, of all bloody things, when I should have been going over technical aspects of the jump and the preparation with him and Henry.

The day before the planned jump we went out on the ferry with all the tourists. I was wearing a large coat with various cables, wires and webbing links tucked underneath. Despite looking, and no doubt behaving, like a bunch of very amateur spies, we didn't seem to attract any undue attention. We had already made a couple of thorough recces of the joint, taking in the scale and the layout of the thing, and I'd already visited the statue some months earlier, with a view to planning a bungy jump. Up close, the Statue of Liberty is one massive lady and my plan involved climbing a rope, firstly up the base, then up her body to her shoulder. The trickiest piece would come at the shoulder, where I had to fire a crossbow with a string attached to the arrow over the torch. I would use this line to walk along the upraised arm, to get to the torch, where I would set up the bungy.

A daunting prospect for sure, but just standing there gave me a real rush of excitement. The statue has a mammoth base which is about 40 metres high, and from there it's another 40 metres to the head of the statue, where the highest public viewing platform is located.

We mingled with the tourists, and once inside the viewing platform in the head of the statue I dropped a weighted piece of fishing line, looped it around a window strut and ran it down to the base of the statue. When we returned at night, I planned to use this line to run a rope up there and haul myself onto the shoulder.

Chris and Henry would be on the terrace below and belay me as I went out to the flame to make the jump. I was going to adopt the same pose as the statue, hanging from the underside of the torch, then drop, bounce around and bugger off. I was planning to do the jump, leave the island and be on a plane that morning out of New York before the footage was even broadcast. At the Eiffel Tower, it was pretty much impossible not to get caught following the bungy jump. But with the Statue of Liberty, one of my major aims was to avoid getting busted after the jump. We figured that if we did it, then got out of there before anyone realised what had happened, then the authorities wouldn't know what to make of it and, as in Paris, they would most probably let the whole thing slide.

As happens pretty much everywhere in the States, there were armed guards wandering about all over the place, so I was looking over my shoulder constantly as I fed out this long fishing line from the viewing platform window. We had some extra helpers in to block the stairwell and stand in the way of cameras while I was doing the job. In one of many stuff-ups, the line tangled, and I could feel the strong wind make a bird's nest of it. I knew instantly that I would need to factor in another half an hour to untangle the thing on the morning of the jump. The whole process of dropping the line can't have taken more than a minute, but we figured from the outset that this was one of the most dangerous times for getting caught. As I needed to open the windows in order to get the line out, I had to figure out a way to unlock the latch. One or two tourists were looking at us oddly and seemed to notice that something was going on, but they soon moved on. Step one complete.

While we were up there, Chris had a wee nosey around and found a fence he could clamber over which led to a maintenance corridor that ran up the statue's arm, all the way to the torch. With all the equipment on me, I could have rigged up a line from the torch right then and there and then simply been belayed up for the jump, thus sparing us the hassle of climbing the actual statue. The only thing stopping us was a padlock on the door that the maintenance guys used to get outside to change the light bulbs. 'Come on, AJ!' Chris said. 'We can use some bolt cutters to get in there and set up the rigging.'

I could understand his eagerness. Cutting the chain would spare us the hassle of dropping the line in a place where people could see us, but I was adamant that we would not damage any property. Bungy jumping was an underground, rebellious activity and if we wanted to stay relatively sweet with the authorities, then we needed to avoid doing anything too criminal. Besides, a key motivation for attempting the jump — just as with the Eiffel Tower — was to express appreciation and admiration for this wonderful structure and defacing it in any way would defeat the whole purpose of the jump.

The next morning at about 2 am, freezing cold and dressed in black, we paddled out to Liberty Island in our little Indian-style canoe. After an hour of pretty unsteady paddling, the three of us plus one television cameraman reached the island. We tucked the canoe under a small delivery wharf out of sight around the back end of the island, and watched for the guards who looped the island every 40 minutes or so. The cameraman went and set up, while the three of us went about climbing up to the six-metre raised terrace that the base of the statue sits upon.

That's where the wheels came off. Because we had been forced to waste so much time during the week getting the equipment and accommodation sorted out, I hadn't given enough thought to making sure that Henry and Chris could get up the ropes onto the base of the statue. I free climbed the five metres or so up to the base and threw down a rope for them to climb up. I was an expert at scaling ropes and I had spent months training outside my window in Paris. I stupidly assumed that these two would also find it a piece of cake, but they just couldn't get the hang of it. I should have been teaching them how to prusik — a basic skill from rock climbing — up a rope during the week instead of running around organising things the production company guys had loused up.

So there I was, leaning over the edge hissing down instructions to Chris and Henry, who were really labouring with heavy packs full of gear. Time was ticking away and every now and then I would see a security guard walk by. Eventually, Chris hauled himself up but by the time Henry got up there, amid much huffing and swearing, it was pretty clear that our opportunity had passed.

All of this had put us more than an hour behind schedule. Here's a bit of brilliant hindsight for you: based on the fact that we hadn't been able to rehearse prusiking, we should have bought a bloody ladder. Once we finally got up to the terrace, we knew we were clear of security, as they only walked around on ground level.

Then I stumbled across stuff-up number two: my fishing line was too short. The line I would use to climb up the 40-metre base was just a few metres out of reach from where I stood. Once again, a ladder was looking like a pretty useful piece of kit. I had seen a ladder down by a little maintenance shed and knew that I could scarper down there easily enough and grab the thing. But what about the guards? Chris's job as lookout was made almost impossible by those blasted walkie-talkies. By the time I got back it would be nearly 5 am. We would have only one hour to do a hell of a lot of work. And even once I reached the lines, I knew they would still need to be untangled. I've never sworn so much in my life.

Eventually light was beginning to show in the sky, and it was obvious that without a miracle we weren't going to get the job done. After some terse words between the three of us, we decided to pull the pin — it seemed certain we would be caught if we continued. We were a forlorn trio as we shimmied down the ropes and trudged back to where the boat was stashed and paddled away to the launch that was waiting for us.

Back on shore, we had to move fast. After an hour's power sleep at the hotel we went back to Liberty Island on the first public boat of the day at 9 am. We were all running on the last of our energy reserves as we headed up the tower to retrieve the lines. Then it was back to the hotel where I made the lines longer.

Wolfing down a bagel, we made it back to the wharf in time to get the last boat that night, returning to the island to set up our lines again.

After a week of frenetic activity and two days with barely any sleep, I was in a near comatose state as I leaned out the window to hurl the line clear from the top viewing platform. That's when stuff-up number three came home to roost. Watching as the line unfurled sweetly — marking the path I would take up the statue the next morning — my eyes followed the fishing line down until they came to rest on a woman at ground level looking back up at me. She was staring at me and I could just make out a look on her face which seemed more curious than surprised. Everything appeared to slow down as she pointed at me and then called over to a guard. Game over.

By the time we got down the stairwell, there were three guards with guns pointed at our heads.

'You guys are either terrorists here to mess with our statue or you're planning to parachute off the thing,' said one, confirming the American flair for overstatement. 'And either way, it ain't gonna happen.'

Apparently, an Aussie bloke had found the same maintenance corridor that Chris Allum had stumbled across on our reconnaissance mission, cut the padlock and base jumped from the torch about a month earlier. These guards were pretty fired up. They took us to the little police station on the island where we were eventually fined $50 and sent on our way.

'Would you like us to take down our line for you?' I asked, trying to be helpful.

'Don't worry. We'll get it down in the morning,' the chief guard said.

Now that raised my eyebrows. The last boat off the island was delayed by an hour waiting for us and as it pulled away I stood with Henry and Chris and looked at the lines still hanging there. Hanging perfectly.

'What do you reckon guys, the lines are hanging perfectly,' I said. 'We could come back tonight.'

When the ferry got to shore, the production company found us a lawyer who warned us that if we were caught making another attempt on the Statue of Liberty, we could expect to serve some jail time; maybe up to three months behind bars and a fine in the region of $5000. Prison wasn't an attractive prospect — I had no desire to be the Bungy Man of Alcatraz — so the three of us had a good long talk about it. It still seemed like a hell of a prospect. What a jump it would be — the footage would be unforgettable.

We ummed and aahed — at one point we even considered jumping the Brooklyn Bridge, but it wouldn't have been the same. Ultimately, all three of us were still fired up to try the Statue of Liberty. I figured that we'd learnt from our first attempt about what to do and what not to do. With the knowledge from that first failed effort tucked away in our minds, I felt that we were better placed to pull it off than we had been when we set out on that first night.

That's always been my approach to failure in general. If

something hasn't worked out, if it's gone a bit pear-shaped, then see what you can learn from the failure and go on to achieve what you set out to do in the first place.

Of course the line that we had run down from the viewing platform was still there.

Hell, maybe I was letting my ego get the better of me, but I had worked so hard on this — sneaking into construction sites in Paris to test the bungy lengths and practise prusiking. The Paris jump had been such a success, and I already had my mind focused on this wonderful helicopter footage of me — little old AJ Hackett bouncing away on a bungy at dawn's early light from the upraised arm of the Statue of Liberty. Awesome.

Anyway, commonsense won the day. We took a vote and the jump never went ahead. And, of course, we never went to jail. Someday I'd like to try it again, but legally.

Of course, these days I reckon it would have to be legal. We live in a different world today — I guess September 11 changed a lot of things, especially in America. It's hard to be so easygoing now. Today, if three blokes were found paddling a canoe out to the Statue of Liberty under cover of darkness, wearing balaclavas and carrying a crossbow, I reckon they'd either be blown out of the water or find themselves wearing orange overalls in Guantanamo Bay in a hell of a hurry.

CHAPTER 6

The magic
formula

The moment I landed back in New Zealand there was a
television interviewer's microphone being pushed into my face,
which was exactly the same situation as when I'd left the country a
few months earlier. On 10 July 1985, 18 months before I jumped off
the Eiffel Tower, French secret agents had blown up the *Rainbow
Warrior*, a Greenpeace ship leading protests against French
nuclear testing in the South Pacific. In an act of state-sponsored
terrorism, frogmen had swum in the Waitemata Harbour to plant
charges beneath this vessel, berthed right on the doorstep of
downtown Auckland. A crew member, Fernando Pereira, died in
the sinking — he was the ship's photographer and ran back into
the darkroom after the first explosion to rescue prints and film
crucial to the Greenpeace cause. He died when a second mine
attached to the hull exploded, finishing off the vessel.

New Zealand police caught two of the bombers trying to flee

the country but the Government was powerless against the might of France to have international justice fully brought to bear on them. France threatened our valuable trade with Europe. Kiwis were outraged and, understandably, there's still some bad blood about it today — it was a foul act from an otherwise friendly state which we had helped out in two world wars. Happily, the actions of the French Government didn't accord with the attitudes, and certainly the charm, of the many French friends I had already made while a guest in their country. Domestically, in New Zealand anti-Gallic feeling at that time was pretty high, helped along by the fact that we spanked the French in the inaugural Rugby World Cup final, played at Auckland's Eden Park in July 1987.

Somehow, in this wave of stick-it-to-the-French sentiment, my leap from the Eiffel Tower came to symbolise little New Zealand's pluck and endeavour in the face of old-world arrogance. Suddenly, bungy jumping had a rebellious, yet patriotic, element to it. I left the country as a carpenter and joiner with a microphone under his nose. I returned as Mr Bungy.

By now I was really starting to tune into the commercial possibilities of bungy — although I still had this idea that it would be just me jumping, not paying clients — and I was in contact with a few agencies and promotions people looking for opportunities to push their products. Sure enough, six months after I arrived, the opportunity arose to jump off the stock exchange building for the opening of the Chase Plaza beneath it. Perhaps it was in questionable taste, given the fact that people failing in share markets elsewhere in the world in decades gone by had occasionally thrown themselves off buildings without the safety of a bungy cord. But the spectacle would be grand and, in many ways, bungy summed up the spirit of optimism prevalent in New

Zealand's commercial sector at the time. They were busy days for share trading, and the image of a man going down, then up, then down, and up again and so on, made a nice metaphor for what went on in the stock exchange itself. This would also fund my next trip to France.

Of course I was more interested in the jump itself. I really wanted to do something special for the New Zealand public. I was determined to get the weights and cord figured out exactly right, so that I could get a nice little hand touch on the surface at the bottom of the jump. This was to be the first time anyone had bungied off a building and that in itself was pretty hairy. It was the first time that I'd done a bungy jump so close to any standing structure — we had always made a point of jumping well clear of the arches and struts beneath a bridge — and as an added worry it was also the first time I'd jumped in front of a massive audience. There was the possibility that I would slam into the sheer glass plates of the building with a huge audience looking on. Pain and humiliation were a distinct prospect. Great.

I set up a slightly extended rigging system so that the bungy cord was connected to a steel frame that we had made up, which jutted out from the building. I was most worried about swinging back on the rebound and into the glass-plated side of the building — it's all very well and good getting a ground touch and then bouncing back up on the bungy, but I was concerned about getting too much inward drift and smashing into one of those thin windows. Because the thin glass windows were edged with razor-sharp aluminium, I decided to attach smooth pieces of rounded wood to the frames, so I wouldn't cut myself on the rebound. Naturally the chippy in me came out, so I commandeered a machine used for raising and lowering window cleaners and used it to get to the windows most likely to be in the impact zone. Even if I hit a window, at least I wouldn't go through it and get cut to shreds. As an added precaution, I bound pieces of thick tough rubber up my arms from my hands to my elbows, so that in the worst-case scenario if I did smash into the windows, I would not sever my arms or arteries. It was going to be a family show, after all.

The key to avoiding hitting the windows as I came back up on the rebound was to not leap too far out from the rooftop. I pretty much had to tuck into a straight drop.

The day of the jump was a beauty. The sun shone and crowds filled the streets below. I learnt later that the other side of the building by Queen Street, the main road through the city centre, was even busier as pedestrians filled the streets hoping for a glimpse of this crazy guy who was going to leap from the stock exchange building — unfortunately they missed it as I jumped from the opposite side.

As the crowd gathered below, I was busy organising things on the rooftop and remained very focused on the mechanics of the jump, so it was only in the moments that I stood on the edge before the actual leap that I had the chance to take in the scene. The cheering masses, the glorious sunshine — what a buzz. I felt so proud that these people had come out to show their support. There was real excitement in the air — no one in the crowd had ever seen a live bungy jump. From down below a chant came up: 'Jump! Jump! Jump!'

I had to shut that out of my mind again and focus on the fall — with the hand touch at the bottom and the glass on the sides, this was an extremely risky and difficult jump. The collective intake of breath from below when I dropped was audible. The hand touch was pretty much perfect and, thankfully, I managed to stay well clear of the windows on the rebound. The crowd were stoked, cheering and whooping: they had seen the local boy come home and do good.

People loved it and the media were all over the jump. There was clearly a market for a bungy business in New Zealand.

In 1987, after returning from my first season of skiing in France, Chris Allum had convinced me to join him in a little venture down at Ohakune, near the ski fields of the central North Island. He and I ran a small ski shop there called New Sensations Supply Company. We were keen, but the money was tight. Real tight. What we were doing was a bit ahead of its time really; we were trying to sell monoskis and snowboards a good six years before everyone really caught onto the buzz about snowboarding. We had seen the monoskis and snowboards on our tours in Europe and felt excited about these new products. We were also doing a bit of business selling European clothing lines we'd picked up on while travelling in Europe. But New Zealand skiers were reluctant to try something new at that time. It's a little galling these days to go to the ski fields and see hundreds of snowboarders zipping around the place — where were these guys when we were trying to sell our stuff?

We were paying some mates a pittance to demonstrate the gear on the hill to try to fire up some interest, but the shop just kept losing money. The pair of us were having to plug our savings into it to keep it all going. I didn't want to keep digging into my pocket to fund this little Ohakune business and nor did Chris. Soon enough, we both realised that we had to clear some debts that had built up on the shop and get out of the place. So Chris convinced me to put on a bungy session, with paying customers being strapped in for a leap off a bridge. I figured that I'd learnt about the importance of keeping control of the jump site from the mass session at Pont de la Caille, so I thought I could manage a session here to clear our bills.

These were to be the first-ever commercial bungy jumps. We called it the New Sensations Bungy Symposium. Up in Silverdale near Auckland, I got New Zealand's premier screen printers, Kiwi Tees, to design and print 100 T-shirts using an image of my silhouette from the Eiffel Tower jump. It's an image that still appears on some of the jump shirts at AJ Hackett Bungy sites around the world today.

My mate Adam Lichtenstein agreed to help and went from demonstrating snowboards to unappreciative Aucklanders one day, to being a bungy expert the next. He remembers the blue mechanics' overalls we all donned to try to look like professionals. 'They were meant to make it look like we were part of a cohesive team and knew what the hell we were doing,' says Adam. 'And it was cold out there — bloody cold. The following year we looked like freezing works labourers with white overalls, Swanndris and red band gumboots.'

We publicised the bungy symposium through the shop and hundreds of people came out to the bridge, which was five minutes out of Ohakune. But no one was jumping — although everyone wanted to jump, and they were all fascinated by what we were doing, they just stood there watching. At the end of the day, we had jumped only six people. At this rate, the bungy that was meant to bail out the ski shop was going to end up costing us even more money. I hadn't paid the T-shirt printer and the bungy

cord itself wasn't cheap.

My mate Guy Jacobson, who runs a flooring firm in Auckland, was in town skiing with his family and dropped in to say hi.

'I've got a problem, Guy. People want to jump but they aren't taking the bait.'

'What are you charging, AJ?'

'It's $100 and for that they get a second jump for free and they can buy the T-shirt for $25.'

'You've got your price structuring all wrong, mate. People don't know what bungy jumping is, so they don't know if they'll like it and if they'll want the second jump. Why not make it $75 for one jump and throw in the T-shirt for free?'

We took Guy's advice and the next day we jumped 60 people; and another 60 jumped the following day. We ran out of T-shirts in the process. It was amazing to see how changing the price structure changed the customers' perceptions so much. The crowds just kept filing through. I had my first physically disabled customer, a blind guy whose capacity to trust us was amazing — further proof that bungy was for everyone. The product hadn't changed one iota from that first day — a single jump still really cost $50, the T-shirt still cost $25, but our business was flying. This is the same pricing structure we started with in Queenstown and it basically still works around the world today. We had found the magic formula.

We sold tickets through the shop and customers loved it. The first symposium was a three-dayer and we later had a ten-day session, which broke the back of our financial problems altogether. It also opened my eyes to a few realities about the commercial possibilities in bungy. When we priced the deal attractively — throwing in a free T-shirt — there was a very viable business model for us to tap into. I started thinking long term: could we feasibly set up bungy sites for a whole season? Or perhaps even longer? And would people continue to pay for the thrill of the jump? The answer, as demonstrated by that ten-day session, was 'hell yes'.

We took the cash we made there and wrapped up our business in Ohakune. A couple of months later I cut a deal with Henry and Chris. I would start the pair of them off at a bungy site each, Henry in Queenstown and Chris at the bridge we used out of Ohakune, and then I'd get a cut of their businesses when they were up and running. A few months later we all drove down to Queenstown to get the thing under way.

Today it gets billed as 'the adventure capital of the world', but when we arrived in Queenstown there was a little rafting, some kayaking, a few jetboat operators and, of course, the skiing and that was about it. The town turned over a nice bit of revenue and visitor numbers kept ticking over. But by and large, it was a scenic holiday destination, and certainly not an extreme one.

I felt confident, however, that the ski culture that had taken to bungying so well at Pont de la Caille and again in the two brief sessions up at Ohakune would show itself again in Queenstown. I figured that the Kawarau Bridge would be a good place to start — it was close to town, nobody was using the bridge and it was right alongside the main road into Queenstown. The bridge was owned by the Department of Conservation (DOC), who were a bit bemused about what I was suggesting, so I had to find a way of convincing them to let us operate on the bridge. The key was to get them on side with something that was good for what they were doing.

I pitched it to them as an opportunity to restore the bridge. DOC got five per cent of the income from every jump off the Kawarau Bridge and that money went into a fund for the restoration of the bridge. There was actually a real need to repair parts of this bridge, it had rotten old beech wood and Australian hardwood along the base of the thing that needed to be replaced. Gradually we smoothed over the safety concerns of some worried-looking local councillors and DOC staff. None of these guys had ever considered the possibilities of the sort of extreme sport tourism that we were advocating. I found the trick was to constantly bring the discussions back to the restoration of the bridge. No one else had any funding to fix the old bridge up: government agencies like DOC were strapped for cash and local councils had a million other things to deal with.

The staff at DOC were the main ones that we had to win over. Right from the beginning, it was obvious that we had to get them on our side. The bridge belonged to them and they could grant access rights to most of the interesting sites around Queenstown. Or they could deny us outright. I knew that the river guide companies were all paying a fairly nominal amount to DOC for using the rivers, so our offer of five per cent for the restoration seemed generous and environmentally sound. It was all money well spent — it kept us sweet with DOC and helped look after some of the really important stuff around New Zealand. There was also the obvious advantage that as long as we were operating on the bridge, we would actually be gaining from its restoration.

We arrived in Queenstown one Saturday afternoon and on the Tuesday we threw a party at Eichardt's pub to announce that we would be open for business the following Saturday, despite not having permission from DOC. It was all seat-of-pants stuff. A friend, Steve Tag, helped me draw up a letter to get permission from DOC, which they granted on the Thursday. About a nanosecond after the consent came in from DOC, I was up there on the bridge hammering a jump platform in place. When we started, the bridge was not far from being in total disrepair. We had to jury-rig a few things to make it safe for foot traffic and hurriedly put in place a walking track from the side of the river back up to the top.

DOC had given us a one-month licence to jump customers from the bridge. A lot of people at the department assumed that we would jump a few tourists, hand them some cash at the end of our month and then get out of town, never to be seen again. But we had plans to keep the operation running and get more licences. At the end of the second week of operations we threw a massive party at Nugget Point, a boutique hotel nearby, to raise more awareness of the restoration of the bridge. We invited the key people from the local council, DOC and other business people from around town. At that stage we had already raised $5000 for the restoration fund, and that just blew DOC away. We had a big cheque drawn up and presented it to them and lots of photos appeared in the local paper. I always talked them up in the press.

If we raised enough money, I knew DOC would continue

extending our licences. When buses full of tourists pulled up
wanting to watch a bungy jump, I would stop the jumps and have
one of our staffers run around with a bucket telling the tourists to
throw in some cash for the restoration project if they wanted to see
a jump.

Within two years, DOC had a couple of hundred grand
in its restoration fund — enough to put the bridge back in
immaculate condition. We instantly became DOC's second-biggest
concessionaires behind the ski fields. Today, the Kawarau Bridge
site still donates a generous proportion of its turnover to DOC and
I'm proud that the money has been used to fund some wonderful
projects throughout New Zealand. The partnership that we
established in the first weeks has proved fruitful for all concerned.

The deal I cut with Henry was that for the first 20 days, the
Kawarau Bridge operation was all mine and I paid him something
like $4 a jump. After that it was Henry's, and I took a cut of the
profits. Later I went to Ohakune and set up Chris there along the
same lines.

My sister Elaine was living in Sydney so I called her up and
invited her to come over and work for us doing the books and
managing the non-operational side of things. We had a big
number-crunching session one night where we sat down over
a few beers to go over the pricing structure. We figured if we
charged $75 a jump and did 50 a day, we would be insanely rich.
But if we charged $75 a jump and did 15 a day, we'd be sunk!

We opened for business pretty much the next day, on
12 November 1988. We were ready to do the first commercial

bungy jumps in Queenstown and, naturally, I was the first one to jump off the Kawarau Bridge. A couple of hundred people arrived to see what all the hype was about. I waved to them as I edged out onto the platform ready to make the first leap. We were using the bungies from Ohakune, because the two bridges were the same height. At least we thought they were.

Right next to the Kawarau Bridge there was a sign reading '44 metres'. All the documentation on the bridge — tourism pamphlets, papers in the DOC office, newspaper articles — said '44 metres'. What they should have said was '44 metres . . . when the river levels are at their lowest'.

So over I go, expecting to get close to the river without actually getting a water touch. Of course, it came as quite a surprise when I disappeared up to my ankles in the fast-moving Kawarau River.

'It's not 44 metres!' I yelled to the guys in the raft as they pulled me down and untied the bungy. With all the spectators cheering what looked like a dramatic success, I sprinted up the stairs, waving and smiling to the crowd.

'Er, fellas,' I whispered, so as not to alarm anyone. 'Let's just pull the old bungy cord up a bit higher for the rest of the jumps and when all the crowds have gone at the end of the day maybe we should measure the bridge.'

We found it was closer to 39 metres from the bridge to the water. From day two onwards we've measured the water levels every day; they can vary by anything up to eight metres.

The people who came to bungy jump with us in those very first days at Queenstown were fantastic. On the first day, there was nothing other than this exciting concept and a lot of bluster we had talked up in the pubs of Queenstown the week before. Most of the customers on the first couple of days were Kiwis and had heard of bungy jumping, but they had no preconceptions about it. They came because they wanted to try something new and brilliant, and they left our site elated. Over the first few weeks as our reputation developed, the element of peer pressure grew. If all the coolest dudes in town had done it, then you had to do it too.

Some of the people who would go on to become the core staff of our business, and indeed the leading figures in the adventure-tourism industry, joined as staff in those early days. Our first jump-master, Kevin Jennings, became a real fixture in the industry and is as safe a pair of hands as you could hope for. On the very first day we were open, a local lad called Glenn Russell — also known as Hippy — was working the raft at the bottom, pulling in the customers after we'd lowered them down and then paddling them ashore. It's a cold job down there, as you're often out of the sun and the water is freezing. Hippy did his first-ever jump at the end of the day: 'It was like the biggest imaginable hit of pure adrenalin. I was amped for hours. I remember going back into town and just raving about it in the pub to anyone who would listen.'

Another who joined us in the early days was Andy Brinsley who had pitched up one day and asked if we would mind if he sold some fruit in the car park. It was fine by us, as we had nothing going on off the bridge itself, other than the old white caravan where Elaine or Caroline would be shivering over a cup of tea and booking people to jump. So Andy shot down the road to Cromwell and bought a whole lot of fruit, then sat there for a few days making a few dollars selling nectarines. One day when we were a bit short staffed, we asked him to help out. He went on from there to become our first general manager, and he and Hippy would later be at the heart of one of the most bizarre twists in our business's history.

Right from the start we did things differently. We stuck up some rudimentary fliers around the town and didn't go through the normal booking agents. Word of mouth was our biggest marketing tool. We really played up the fact that the site only had a 30-day operating licence and the days were ticking past, so if you wanted to be in then this could be your only chance. There was an underground feel to what we were doing that appealed immensely to young travellers, so right away we found that foreigners were the biggest market. We didn't have a formal structure — when we had said goodbye to the last jumpers at the end of each day, we would take the cash float and bury it beneath a concrete block on the far side of the river.

We filmed people jumping and then played the videos that night down at Eichardt's Hotel, an old pub on the waterfront in town. The buzz spread quickly. Someone had the bright idea of a nude day, with a free jump for anyone brave enough to jump in the nude. We thought we might get one or two, but it seemed like pretty much all of Queenstown turned up for their free jump.

One of the best marketing coups was the T-shirt deal that we came up with. It was simple: if you completed your bungy jump, you got a free T-shirt. If you didn't complete the jump, no T-shirt. Day-glo colours were in and you could see these T-shirts from 300 metres away. The shirts became a talking point and it was sort of a macho thing to have one — proof that you'd completed the jump. It was almost a tribal thing: having completed the ritual you got to wear the feather in your cap. We even had people offering to pay for a jump just to get the T-shirt, but we always stuck to our guns, which of course added to the value of the shirt for the people who had earned them.

After a week, a month and even after several months, established operators in town would see us in the street and express surprise that we were still in business: 'Hello fellas. When are you going back to Auckland?'

After the first 30 day licence, DOC gave us two consecutive 60 day licences, followed by a five year licence. Finally, they presented us with a 66 year deal.

In the beginning, people didn't think we mattered. Nobody grew up in New Zealand thinking that jumping off a bridge with a bit of elastic tied to your feet was a natural thing to do. Mind you, when we eventually opened a site in Normandy in France, the locals thought we were Martians.

Queenstown journalist Philip 'Scoop' Chandler remembers the locals' attitude to the bungy business that had sprung up in their happy little hamlet: 'You guys were seen as some sort of wide boys — rocking into town with this brand-new thing that seemed pretty much destined to kill someone within a few weeks. Each night the bungy boys were down there at Eichardt's promoting it and getting people out there for the next day and it was just a sensation. But a lot of people never thought it would last beyond that first season.

'One thing that added to that impression was the fact that you guys had these short-term concessions to use the bridge. I think that fact — the short concessions — maybe showed that some people just didn't think you'd last. And it certainly made it look like DOC and the council didn't think you would last.

'When you saw the site in those early days, it didn't really inspire confidence in the longevity of the operation. You had this clapped-out old bus that was being used as a sort of office. So you had to wonder, what's the business model and how's it all being run?'

Truth is, there was a lot of stuff we did poorly from a business point of view, but the sheer weight of demand from customers ensured that we were fine. The product was too cool and too unique to fail.

Andy Brinsley remembers a client who summed up the strange appeal of our product. 'We were sitting in the caravan, playing cards and drinking tea on a particularly slow day, when this guy came by on a pushbike. He was a European kid doing a cycling tour of New Zealand. He stopped to say hello and we got chatting. Now, he had never heard of bungy — he had no idea what we were all about. We had to explain the whole concept to him. He stands there listening to us with his bike at his side and wearing this blank expression. Then he says: "Okay, I'll do it."

'He jumped, loved it, hopped on his bike and rode away. It all seemed kind of surreal. I remember standing there watching this guy cycle off and thinking that if people would pay good money to do this thing with absolutely no prior knowledge of what it even was, then we were definitely onto a very good thing.'

At the end of that first summer season, Henry and I had done really well out of the Kawarau Bridge, but he planned to shut down for the winter and then consider whether to return the next summer. I was adamant that we should stay open. The fire was hot, the town would fill with ski tourists and the initiative was ours. If we went away now, then by the time we returned next summer all sorts of competitors would be crawling over that bridge earning money that could be ours.

Eventually I talked Henry round. He could see the business sense in what I was saying, however it was definitely a gamble — sales for all non-skiing Queenstown tourism operators traditionally dropped off over the winter months, so we braced ourselves to take a hit. But the numbers were really good. That was when I knew that bungy had found its home in Queenstown as a 365-day-a-year operation. We got through that first winter with reasonable numbers — just enough to show that there was a solid financial base for what we were doing.

So we built on that financial base, and continued to build. At the end of the first summer we built the first bungy centre out there. It was a pretty basic structure, just solid enough to keep staff and spectators dry and warm when it rained or snowed, but it meant we could get rid of the crusty old white caravan and the beat-up old bus from which we had been doing our sales and bookkeeping. We also built the first secure viewing deck on the site as, up until that point, we had just marked off the edge of the cliff with some fencing wire. With growing numbers of people standing on the side of the cliff, it seemed prudent to build something to keep them away from the edge. This ensured that our main winter market customers — who we figured would be wealthier and more conservative — wouldn't fall over and get their nice après-ski gear wet and muddied.

As soon as we could afford to, we tried to create a really

nice physical environment out at the site. When we started in Queenstown, a lot of the rafting operators had nice polished shop fronts in the town itself, but when you went out to the sites where their boats were launched from everything was all run down and they did nothing to take care of the environment around them.

Elaine remembers the early buzz about the site and our business around the town: 'They were great days — it was the late eighties and you could do anything basically. We went out seven nights a week. Eight nights a week! When we got there the river guides, the rafting guys, were the kings of the town, so when we kicked off and got pretty much all the attention, some of them were a bit stunned. It's not often that someone invents a new tourism market.'

Each week the staff would go for a meal at a Japanese restaurant called Minami Jujisei. All the bungy crew would turn up and by the end of the night there'd be a $3000 sake bill. We would all be tucked away in a room out the back of the restaurant, drinking and eating — and drinking a bit more. And drinking even more still. It was mayhem. At the end of the night, the staff would discreetly slide open the rice paper door and they'd just lean in and place the vacuum cleaner there. We'd tidy up as best we could, pay for the damage and return the next week.

Hippy remembers those nights well: 'We pretty much used to destroy the place on a weekly basis. They'd just put the repair bill underneath the bill for the menu.'

On the business side of things, we were learning all the time. The payment system in the early days saw staff earning their cash per jump — just like the deal I had cut with Henry and Chris right at the outset. The more jumpers, the more cash they earned. It was a great way to build enthusiasm in the staff but after a couple of months it became apparent that we were going to go bankrupt if we kept it up. We were paying so damn much to the staff that we weren't going to have enough to cover the overheads. It was my sister Elaine who cottoned on to it one day when she was doing the books and had to write herself a cheque for $8000 for about a fortnight's work. She rang me and said: 'Hang on, AJ. I've done the same amount of work as last month. This has got to change.'

This was when AIDS was really becoming a major issue in people's minds all around the world, so there was a global shortage of latex as condoms were being bought up all over the world. We noticed that rubber was getting scarce — there was a worldwide shortage. The fact that people were shagging safely was making it hard for us to get our cords. In Queenstown we ended up taking used bungies and stripping out the cords. In a 20-cord bungy the middle two might be worn and broken but the outside ones were fine, so we'd strip them out and get more use from them in a new bungy. We also recognised that we needed to redesign the bungy ends to get a frictionless component that would not wear away at the rubber so much. With this in place, bungies now last anywhere between 400 and 600 jumps, increasing their life fourfold.

We had run-ins with other companies who thought they would try to open up and copy what we were doing. Many people looked at what we were doing and thought it was some sort of licence to print money. And our turnover was certainly good. One lot, who had experience running a successful rafting company, thought they would have a go at opening on the other side of the Kawarau

Bridge — so our jump-masters would be working back-to-back with their jump-masters. We fought that every step of the way as they applied to DOC for a consent to build on the bridge with us. We managed to block them out.

But we knew there was no way we could stop people from setting up in competition eventually. What we were worried about was someone coming in with no safety standards at all and killing a customer, because that would wipe out the whole trade. Bungy is all about perceived risk and it's fair to say that in those early days some people involved in the tourism industry around Queenstown were pretty much sitting back and waiting for us to kill someone, then piss off out of town. A death in the first season would have spelt the end of the industry.

Andy Brinsley was the first staff member that we took away from the operational side of things. We took him off the bridge and got him working in more of a front line role, doing marketing and looking at getting more business out to the site. At the time one of the biggest issues for us was the consent from DOC. We were still operating on these 60-day licences. We were still beholden to DOC, who could in theory have pulled the pin on us at any time. It was a major worry for us, as we were starting to invest a bit of money in the business and the site. Andy knew a lot of the DOC guys from his university days, when he had worked with them in the holidays, so he was well placed to oil the wheels there. He also had the job of securing our first long-term licence. Taking Andy away from tying ropes and manning operations on the bridge and putting him into other things full-time marked the beginning of some very hectic growth for the company.

He remembers the gradual changes in the way our operation looked: 'We were becoming more established and looking like a professional tourism outfit. Then we got the five-year licence and we all partied for about five days to mark that. It really did feel as though we had just been granted a licence to print money. Five years simply seemed like an unimaginable length of time.

'I felt really fortunate to be a part of it and learn so much. You don't get too many chances to be involved in a phenomenon. Henry and AJ were both really focused on quality and presenting a professional image.'

The five year licence was also the ultimate expression of faith from DOC — we had won the locals over. With the five year licence in the bag, we needed to get some responsibility and shape into this wild and crazy thing, so Andy got to work on a long-term business model. The next major priority was to sort out a Code of Practice. By this time Hippy was our operations manager, meaning that he was responsible for the running of the actual jump site, and we had him working on the code with Standards New Zealand.

A few months after we opened, I had begun work on a draft Code of Practice for the industry. It was later to become the AS/NZS5848, the standard operating procedure for bungy sites. For now, though, it was Hippy's job to push it through.

'The idea of a Code of Practice served us well,' says Hippy. 'On the one hand it made the industry safer — and in the early days that was absolutely crucial. You could have ended up with a blood-bath as these fly-by-night operators set up and shoved people off without really knowing what they were doing. The overall effect would have been that customers, tourism operators and ultimately the government would lose faith in bungy jumping. We could all have been shut down. So a good solid Code of Practice staved off that possibility.

'The second thing is that we made the Code of Practice bloody hard to live up to — you had to have so many jumps under your belt, and go through pretty rigorous testing. And that made it really hard for competitors to get going, which was obviously all good for us.'

The safety thing was sort of a double-edge sword for us. Obviously, we felt worried that we could be closed down if there were too many accidents and fatalities around the world. There's also the fact that people didn't actually want to die — if they did want to die, they would have been jumping off bridges without the addition of our rubber band around their feet. But if there were accidents, then it made those who had done a jump feel prouder of having done one. It's all about perceived risk.

As Hippy puts it: 'People want perceived risk, but they don't want to be hurt. If they see in the newspaper that someone has died bungy jumping they'll be quick to tell their mates "I've bungy jumped".'

By this time I was living permanently in France and racing back to Queenstown to sort out DOC hearings and help out from time to time, but with the domestic foothold established it was time to start looking for new pastures.

CHAPTER 7

Myths and
science

I t's fair to say that there has been some fogginess about how bungy jumping was invented for rather a long time. In fact as the years have gone by, I've become more and more foggy about the details myself. One of the great myths of the bungy industry is that I invented it all by myself — like some wild visionary; another tale has it that Henry and I were inspired to create our rubbery game after travelling to see the original vine jumpers in Vanuatu.

These myths have certainly done me and my business a lot of good over the years. But the truth, as I spelled out at the start of this book, is that I was introduced to bungy by my mate Chris Sigglekow. And I'd like to acknowledge publicly the debt that I — along with anyone else who has ever enjoyed the bungy thrill — owe to Chris. But make no mistake. Bungy as the world knows it would not have happened if I hadn't found myself tumbling off the Greenhithe Bridge. I've stamped my mark on this sector of the adventure-tourism industry — created it even — and am proud to have done so.

Full credit to Chris Sigglekow for introducing me to it. But before Chris came along there were three other men called David Kirke, Chris Baker and Ed Hulton — marvellous men; mad as snakes. These guys were among the founding members of the Oxford University Dangerous Sports Club — the original madcap English guys. They bought into — and perpetuated — the idea of the adventurous upper-class gent pushing new frontiers. Through men like Sir Walter Raleigh, Captain Scott and countless officers at war, there's a strong English history of pushing at challenging frontiers. They saw footage from the 1960s made by David Attenborough and a BBC film crew of the land divers of Pentecost Island in Vanuatu. In the eyes of the Oxford undergraduates, Attenborough's footage of young men leaping from tall, flimsy-looking wooden platforms with vines tied to their ankles was stunning. That footage, combined with the innate adventurousness of the Oxford pioneers, led to a remarkable connection: rubber.

The OUDSC rounded up some old parachute harnesses and a hefty supply of rubber strands and on April Fools' Day, 1979, they headed for the 76 metre Clifton Suspension Bridge in Bristol. Now this was true courage — these guys carried out some rudimentary tests, but they had no real idea how the rubber would act, if it would snap or how far it would stretch. They had the foolhardy bravery that has seen Englishmen charging around the world seeking adventure for centuries — and they had style.

Every dangerous stunt the club members engaged in was done while wearing formal dress and with an abundant supply of champagne — hence the dress code for my leap off the Eiffel

Tower. At the moment that the four of them leapt from the bridge, modern bungy jumping was born. Of course, the jumpers were arrested after their leap, but they were enthused and went on to do more jumps around the UK and ultimately jumped off the Golden Gate Bridge in San Francisco and the Royal Gorge Bridge in Colorado — at 320 metres, the world's highest suspension bridge. When these guys jumped off the Golden Gate Bridge, they hadn't figured out how to get back up again, so they had to hang there for an hour while friends up on the bridge went looking for bits of rope to lower down to them. By now the media was taking an interest in what they were doing, and television footage from the jumps in the US was beamed around the world.

This was totally crazy stuff. All they wanted to do was defy death — to have a go and see what would happen. The Oxford lads were the links that sparked up bungy, connecting the new, adventure-based Western activity with the original vine jumpers on the Pentecost Islands. I've thanked David Kirke for his role in gifting this inspirational thing to the world.

The Oxford guys were all real characters and when they'd had their fun with bungy they threw themselves into other extreme activities. They pioneered base jumping with parachutes off cliff tops and high-rise buildings and, memorably, a member of the club once played a grand piano as it skidded down the ski slopes of Saint Moritz, in Switzerland. They were also among the first to have a go at zorbing, which involves a pretty hair-raising (and nausea-inducing) ride inside a large inflatable ball that is pushed down a hill. A few commercial operators later sprang up in New Zealand, so that's another activity that our adventure-tourism industry owes to 'Captain' Kirke.

In a more recent and very sad footnote, a club member made

a move that would be the OUDSC's boldest and, ultimately, its most tragic. With only Kirke left from the original bungy pioneers, another founding member called David Aitkenhead carried on the club. Somehow a couple of people decided that firing people from a trebuchet — a medieval catapult device that used a sling and a tonne of lead to put extra momentum on the object being thrown — would be a good idea. Aitkenhead built one of these things that in times past were used to fire objects over castle walls. They did extensive testing to get the weights and ranges right and, in fairness, were probably as accurate as you could hope to be. When they were satisfied with the testing, they erected a large net and moved into throwing people. I saw David in 2000 and my jaw dropped when he told me what they were up to. I told him straight away it was inviting disaster and urged him to get the OUDSC to reconsider what it was doing. He seemed to feel it was out of his hands.

There were, predictably, minor accidents. The injuries were mostly minor: bruises and twisted ankles as fliers hit the net. In 2000 an OUDSC member, Aitkenhead's girlfriend Stella Young, bounced straight out of the net onto the ground and broke her pelvis.

Tragedy struck when a nineteen-year-old Oxford University student Kostydin Yankov missed the net completely and died from his injuries. Aitkenhead and his fellow catapult designer, Richard Wicks, were acquitted of manslaughter.

A few months after the Golden Gate Bridge jump, Chris Sigglekow was working as a television editor in Auckland when a friend in

the office mentioned the amazing footage. Chris hadn't seen it
— and to this day he still hasn't — but something about the story
his colleague told him got Chris thinking. He was going down to
Nelson for the Christmas period where he knew the Pelorus Bridge
would be ideal to have a go at jumping.

He paid a visit to the Engineering Department at Auckland
University, where he met a professor who was an expert on
rubber, to try to figure out what sort of thing he needed.

'Do you realise, Mr Sigglekow, that there is a very wide array of
different rubbers out there?'

Chris looked blankly at the professor. 'Er, no. I was kind of
thinking about using that tough sort of rubber you get on spear
guns that you use in scuba diving. You know the stuff I mean?'

A resigned look spread across the professor's face. 'What are
you on?' he asked. The professor explained that the rubber Chris
was referring to, although coarse to the touch, pretty strong in
the hands and well-suited to spear fishing, would not be reliable
enough for humans jumping off bridges.

'You want to use pure latex rubber,' he said. 'And unless you
go for that I'm not interested in being involved. I don't want to help
you jump to your death.'

That's what led to Chris's big hallelujah moment. The professor
directed him to an Auckland firm called Kinnears which imported
high-quality rubber from Malaysia, mostly for the yachting market
and for industrial applications. Chris walked into their warehouse
and there were boxes and boxes of this stuff, selling for about $20
a box.

'That was a major point,' says Chris. 'All of a sudden it went
from "can-we-do-it?" to "can-do".'

With his supply of top-quality latex and an old parachute

harness in tow, Chris made his trip to the Pelorus Bridge in January 1980, taking along a mate for help. Like the Oxford boys, he also carried out a couple of fairly rudimentary tests, filling a large sack with rocks found at the riverside and tying the thing onto the bungy cord.

'If the sack of rocks goes okay then I should be fine,' Chris assured his friend. So the pair heaved this weighted sack over the side of the bridge.

'Are you sure this is the right weight?' asked his mate. 'It feels a bit heavy.'

'She'll be right,' said Chris, as the thing suddenly dropped like, well, a sackful of stones.

The pair leaned out for a closer look at the test run. Friends were waving from the riverbanks. The sack of rocks hammered straight into the water where the base of the sack simply ripped open under the pressure of the falling rocks. Suddenly the end of the bungy was weightless, and the bungy itself became a large lethal whip — a deadly shanghai — heading straight up to the pair leaning over the bridge.

For an instant Chris and his mate froze before they threw themselves out of the way and the cord whipped straight past where their heads had been.

Lying face down on the bridge, Chris and his mate gingerly looked up once the bungy cord had settled down. Chris said: 'That went pretty well. I'm going next.'

'No way, mate! We need to do another test.'

'There's no way I'm walking all the way down there to pick up all those rocks — it's me next or nothing!'

'Well I'm not helping you to kill yourself,' said his mate, storming off the bridge.

Chris smiled and started strapping himself into the parachute harness which brought his mate back out on to the bridge.

'If you're going to insist on killing yourself I might as well make sure your harness is done up properly.'

The Pelorus Bridge is about a ten-metre jump and Chris figured that even if the bungy didn't work, he'd still be able to handle the fall into the water. Local kids made the jump often enough, and they did it unaided.

Chris remembers: 'I hit the water so bloody hard, that the webbing on the harness ripped into me and left my torso bruised for about a week or so.'

Chris went straight under the water. Maybe three metres down, before the line hit full stretch and ripped him back out again, jerking him about halfway back up to the top of the bridge. Drenched and elated he cheered and waved to friends standing on the riverbank with cameras.

The fact that the rubber cord pulled him out of the water was enough to confirm for Chris that with a bit more grunt and mathematics applied, it could do the business. Chris did three jumps that day, then packed the cord away and forgot about it for six years.

Later, while I was setting up AJ Hackett sites in Queenstown and then around the world, Chris travelled through the US, where he got involved with a high-dive show that was part of a travelling trapeze troupe. Chris would take a seat in the audience for the trapeze show and, at one point during the performance, the ground announcer would say there was a winning ticket beneath one of the seats that would entitle the holder to a free bungy jump. Everyone would scramble to look under their seats and of course the ticket was always beneath Chris' seat. He would then put on his best Southern accent and holler: 'Why it's me!'

For the performance, Chris' name was Billy Bob (pronounced Bawb). 'Ahm between jawbs right now,' he would tell the ground announcer before being whisked up to the crane platform for the jump. To the amazement and horror of the crowd, in a bit of pre-arranged drama Chris would 'accidentally' pull the jump-master off the platform with him. Of course the two were wired up for a safe tandem bungy.

The knots, ties and techniques that Chris and I started to use when we were jumping off the Greenhithe Bridge still pretty much form the mechanics of the industry today. The original strands of rubber that we used to buy from Kinnears in Auckland were pencil thin and vulcanised together. You could stretch an individual strip and break it easily enough. Breaking two strips was harder and breaking three was positively difficult. By the time Chris and I had bound 20 or 30 of these strands together on the banks under the Greenhithe Bridge, we had an incredibly tough bungy cord. These days the bound-together strands are known as 'wraps'.

Pretty much the last stage in the development of these bungy cords came from my French mate Denys. He took the cords I had shown him and added the finishing touch: the French wrap. Basically it involves a series of latex strips which wrap and tie diagonally down the full length of the bigger cord, preventing rough pieces from poking out and generally keeping the whole thing tidier. We used to just tie some elastic at irregular intervals along the length of the cord. Denys ran these strips criss-crossing down the length of it and that was it — the basic technique for making a bungy cord as we developed it, which is still in use. A couple of the knots and the counterbalance systems on the platform have been tweaked and modified but the mechanics of the cord itself are as simple as ever.

Rubber is an amazing material. Most people give no thought to how tough the stuff is. Look at the tyres on your car. You're braking and turning, the tyres are exposed to salt spray, sun, rain — everything — and they're bloody fine. They're good for 30,000 km. Rotate them once in a while and they'll last for even longer. We built a business empire out of the stuff.

Yet in the early days, we didn't really know all that much about what made the latex work. It seemed entirely possible that one day you'd jump and the bungy cord would just evaporate. At some point they had to snap, surely? In actual fact, they don't fail like that at all — they just slowly degrade. The strands on the inside of the bungy cord go first, one or two of them may even break, but the outside invariably holds.

At AJ Hackett Bungy we have commissioned lengthy academic studies and reports in New Zealand from the now-defunct Department of Scientific and Industrial Research explaining the where and the why of how the rubber works. The test that impressed me the most involved a bunch of lads, a tractor and a stout fence post.

Early on when Chris Sigglekow and I were jumping in Auckland we teamed up with a mate, Alec Padcoe, and this guy from the Department of Science and Industrial Research to do some testing. We hired a tractor and hooked it up to a simple eighteen-strand bungy cord fixed to a post. We stretched the cord to twice its length, then three times, and so on. We eventually managed to snap it at almost seven times its length with the tractor revving heavily. It was staggering to see the strength of this rubber. When we hooked the tractor up to a 24-strand cord, the wheels of the tractor spun on the tarseal. That's pretty much the type of cord you'd use on a big guy jumping from a regulation commercial bungy site. This type of cord has been used by us for almost two decades. The equipment we use today gives us a great margin for safety: the minimum breaking strain of any component in our system is 2200 kilograms. The lowering ropes which guide clients down after a successful jump can bear up to 4000 kilograms.

The way we operate on the tower itself hasn't changed much in all these years, either. On the site we will always have one, and generally two, jump-masters whose job it is to make sure the operation is running properly on the jump platform itself. A good jump-master can read someone's personality like a psychologist, tie knots like a sailor and — most importantly — keep customers at ease. They can also gauge someone's weight at a glance. The customers are all weighed before they move onto the jump platform and their weight is written on their hands. Once on the platform, they are guided to the 'heavy side' or the 'light side'. We have found over the years that 75 kilograms is the average weight for people in the Western world, so that's our cut-off point. There will be a heavier bungy cord operating for the big folk and a lighter one for the smaller customers. By adding cords we can jump much heavier people and do tandem or multiple jumps at the same time. The biggest customer we have had to date was a 247 kilogram customer off our Las Vegas tower.

The bungy cord is generally attached to the platform by two ropes — one is the shock cord, which takes the initial load, and the other is the lowering rope. The jump-master will lower the cord by one metre for every five kilograms that the jumper weighs under the maximum weight range for that particular cord. For example, if a 65 kilogram person is jumping on the light cord which has a maximum load of 75 kilograms, the ropes will be lowered two metres — one metre for every five kilograms. This formula is good for a jump of up to approximately 60 metres. But as the jump gets higher, the equation changes. For example on a 100-metre jump, the weight change is only 2.5 kilograms for a metre, so the need for precision on big jumps is even greater.

We want everyone at AJ Hackett Bungy to experience the same length of jump. It pisses me off to see bungy operators who have their clients finish 15 metres clear of the water on a 40 metre jump — where's the value for money in that? It's also dangerous, because if there is an equipment failure, the jumper will fall from a greater height.

The only variable in all of this is the way in which a person jumps from the deck. Once the client is standing on the edge of the platform, the psychologist in the jump-master has to figure out what kind of dive to expect — straight out with confidence or drop like a stone with a yelp. Dropping straight off the platform will take a jumper lower down.

The jump-master will add half a metre of cord if the jumper is likely to leap outwards. Likewise, if the customer is looking nervous and seems unlikely to do anything more than plummet shrieking, then the jump-master will raise the bungy cord by half a metre. It's also at this point that the jump-master has to consider whether or not the jumper wants to make a water touch or not and factor this into the equation.

A really good jump-master can get pretty much pinpoint accuracy. 'You want a water touch, mate?' they'll ask. 'Which finger?'

CHAPTER 8

Taking care of
business

In the three or four years after we set up in New Zealand, bungy spread through the Western world like wildfire. The international growth of bungy was spectacular, and my efforts to stay ahead of the game over the past two decades have been taxing to say the least.

Within a year of us launching our New Zealand operations, a few bungy companies were operating from cranes in California. Bungy sites — mostly temporary ones — began to pop up across the United States, and my mates in France were already doing occasional crane-jump sessions. People saw what we were doing and thought it looked incredibly easy, so they went off and tried to set up for themselves. We knew what was going on, how popular bungy was proving to be and how important it was to expand out of New Zealand quickly. About 80 per cent of our market was foreign, so I wanted to push into those areas before all the fly-by-night operators got in there and ruined it for us.

We didn't want to be tainted by these operators who had no idea and were just in it for a quick buck. My greatest fear was that people with no inkling of safety values would come in looking for easy money and end up killing people or causing serious injury. My greatest fear was realised.

Pretty much the first place we looked to expand into was Sydney. With things going from strength to strength in New Zealand, we naturally looked across the Tasman as a sound area for growth. It all made perfect sense: similar countries, similar employment and business environments and — most importantly — similar hordes of young adventurers passing through looking for exciting times.

In 1989 we found a nice site in an area called Picton, just out of Sydney. We built a fantastic set-up, trained the crew and started some heavy-duty promotions around the city, tapping into the market of young travellers. We really threw ourselves into it, desperate to make our first step into the global market a good one. We spent a lot of money developing our site on the edge of a river among the gum trees; sharp offices, a tidy garden, a brand new car park and all the trappings of a bold new business.

With the Saturday of our grand opening approaching everything looked good for a successful launch. We were all looking forward to the Saturday . . . that is until Wednesday came.

On the Wednesday before we were to open, another operator — headed by the same people who had already had trouble setting up in New Zealand — loused up the whole bungy concept for everyone looking to set up in Australia. They were also trying to get a foothold in the Sydney market and they lined up a dramatic jump to announce their presence. Unlike our enterprise, they were all drama and no nous. For their big launch they had a former Miss Australia, Natalie McCurry, perform a tandem jump over Sydney Harbour with one of their crew members.

In a nutshell, they stuffed up. Poor old ex-Miss Australia hit the surface hard, ploughing straight through about two metres of water and whacking into the sand at the bottom. That's a lot of pain. The next day bungy jumping was banned in Sydney and across all of New South Wales. Thanks a heap guys.

Essentially what happened was that her bungy wasn't hooked up properly on the deck. Somewhere in setting up the system, her cord was not attached to the rigging. Thankfully she was attached to a member of the crew who jumped with her, otherwise she would have hit the water in a freefall. The problem is sometimes you get a spunky woman on the deck and an inexperienced jump-master will use his wrong head for thinking with. He gets distracted and doesn't do his job properly. It was only because a staff member jumped with her, hugging her nice and tight — well she was a former Miss Australia — that she survived, because as her line ran on he pretty much broke her fall. Still he couldn't break her fall completely and she hit the water at a fair velocity. A cracked collarbone and some time in a neck brace represented pretty good fortune for her.

High-profile accidents do the business no favours at all, and to have something like this go belly-up, with a minor celeb coming close to death as the media looks on is about as bad as it gets. We went blue in the face telling council officials, cops and the press that we had nothing to do with the people who had stuffed up and that we were safe operators — but to no avail. Bungy was banned in New South Wales — just two days before we were due to open. If a jet plane crashed, you wouldn't shut down all the jet airlines.

Drinking traditional champagne prior to jumping the Eiffel Tower. Sori watching for security.

BELOW: Ready to jump — Eiffel Tower, Paris

ABOVE: Pre-jump drinks on the Auckland Stock Exchange roof. From left: Steve, Henry, Susie, Carol and Mac.

BELOW: Chris and I looking proud on the shop roof with our sign. Chris's old saying was 'A business without a sign is a sign of no business' — we made a monster!

RIGHT: *During the first days of commercial operation in Ohakune.*

ABOVE: *The Ohakune team — Adam, Dazz, Mark and Chris.*

ABOVE: DOC about to collect their first cheque, Kawarau Bridge, November 1988.

BELOW: Elaine playing receptionist behind a card table during our first week of operations, Kawarau Bridge, 1988.

RIGHT: *Henry van Asch and Caroline, Kawarau Bridge behind the caravan.*

ABOVE: *Caroline's first jump, Ohakune 1987.*

Early crew shot, Eichardts Bar, Queenstown.

BELOW: Me, Henry van Asch and Jerry Honneck having fun celebrating another company birthday.

Somehow bungy was different. Go figure.

Our case in New South Wales wasn't helped by an absurd story that came about after an Aussie policeman on holiday in Queenstown did a water touch on a bungy jump at Kawarau, and hit the surface pretty hard. He came up with two black eyes and, human nature being what it is, word quickly got around in Oz that bungy jumping would ruin your retinas. The theory was that the twang as the bungy cord whipped you back up would jolt the inside of your head, stretching your retinas. Absurd. In fact in a bungy jump, you will only pull a gravitational force of 2.5G to 3G — less than you would pull aboard an average roller-coaster. Bungy is a mind-expanding experience not an eye-shattering one. But when you're trying to bring something new to people, something they've never encountered before, your first problem is getting them past fear of the unknown. We eventually had to commission research at Canterbury University to prove categorically once and for all that bungy jumping did not cause retina damage. Truth is, a well-executed bungy is no more traumatic for the body than slamming the brakes on hard in a car.

So goodbye to our lovely, AU$250,000 bungy site, with its expansive — and expensive — premises and car park. We'd spent thousands setting up and put in loads of time and effort, and we didn't get to do a single commercial jump. Still, waste not, want not. We had to pack up the operation, so we salvaged all the cords, shackles and bits and pieces and sent them off to Queenstown. Best of all, we took the supply of T-shirts that had been printed, ready to be sold to successful jumpers, and we printed 'Banned in Sydney' on them, and sold them at our Cairns operation when we opened up there six months later. The Queensland locals loved it.

With the ban in place, we had an opening and closing party for our mates and some of our suppliers and partners in the venture. We got in a few jumps for fun then, sadly, we packed up the bungy adventure in Sydney.

The ban in Sydney was removed five years later. Some years after it was lifted, I looked into the possibility of opening a bungy site from a cable car operation in a national park area just out of Sydney. But, wouldn't you know it, when the ban on bungy was put into place in New South Wales it was also written into the rules for the state's national parks. No one got around to changing those rules when the general ban was lifted. It's amazing to consider the follow-on effects from that one stuff-up on a sunny day on a bungy platform in Sydney and it shows you how attention to the small things today — the operational matters — is what secures your future in any trade.

Sydney was out of our system, but Australia was still to be the first international step for AJ Hackett Bungy. I had some guys wanting to take a franchise option in Cairns. They would open there, set up the site, run it according to my specifications and pay for the privilege. Brilliant. The key was that we would control their standards — I recognised early on the potential for people to die at the hands of dodgy operators and was determined not to let that happen under my name.

These guys in Cairns had a great site in the rainforest just north of the city, next to a site earmarked for the new James Cook University in Smithfield, and I was confident they would operate the set-up properly.

At about the same time that the Cairns site was opening, we got into a site in Normandy in France; Europe being our next biggest market. I was living in France at the time and thus began a constant theme in my life for the next few years — jetting from France to Australia and New Zealand several times a year, with odd jaunts to the States and Asia, to keep all the balls in the air. In fact the jetting about is still a constant theme in my life today — there would be few people alive as adept at sleeping in an economy class airline seat as I am, while racking up 300,000 kilometres of travel a year.

In the immediate days after Queenstown had launched so successfully, I think perhaps we were a bit naive, thinking that everything we touched would turn to gold like it had back at the Kawarau Bridge. And if it didn't turn to gold immediately, then we sort of thought it would all end up pretty marvellous soon enough. She'll be right. Bungy can't fail. We've got the golden touch. We hadn't had the experience of a bungy site going belly-up on us.

We learnt real fast in Cairns, where we had a couple of franchise holders who had found this property which they planned to turn into a bungy site at a total cost of about AU$400,000. They cobbled together about AU$200,000 and figured they could hold off the creditors until the cash flow started to roll in. Trouble is it took a lot longer for the cash flow to really fire up than they'd figured. And, as I found out afterwards, the clincher was that it actually cost closer to AU$800,000 to set up the site — and it still needed work. By the time they got trading, they were already swimming upstream. It was under-capitalised and although the business was going okay, it was nowhere near strong enough for them to service that massive debt.

Before long the wolves were at the door and when the receiver was appointed, the landlords stepped in pointing out a special clause in the lease that meant all fixed assets would become their property. All the liquidators got were some computers and office equipment. I didn't want to see the beautiful site and all the hard work go to waste, so we made a deal with the landowners. Henry and I brought in my sister Elaine, and our key managers Adam Lichtenstein, Hippy and Andy Brinsley, to raise money to buy the place. As a sweetener, Henry and I gave the others one per cent each of the AJ Hackett Bungy group to come on board.

There was an uproar because there were a lot of creditors who were left out of pocket and two other groups had formed to try to take over the site. But we had a deal with the landowners and we were the best bungy operators in the world. Sometimes in business you have to move fast to secure a deal, and that may leave some people feeling aggrieved. I could not afford to let this site — our first AJ Hackett Bungy enterprise outside of New Zealand — fall flat on its face. We tied up our deal to take back the Cairns operation about an hour before the whole thing was to be put up for auction.

One thing about my international bungy sites is that I always seem to find myself dealing with some odd characters and bizarre situations as far as local investors, business partners and landlords go. The situation was no different in Cairns. My Asia–Pacific manager, Adam Lichtenstein, says: 'Our landlord situation is very interesting everywhere we go. If you think about the activity we're involved in, you've got to be a fairly unusual character to let this sort of business be set up on your property. As Kiwis we tend to be up for pretty much anything. But for foreigners it takes a special breed.'

Our former manager in Cairns, Evan Bloomfield, guided the

site out of its early troubles and today it's a triumph. There's a great team in there led by Luke Johnson. They operate on a beautiful site recognised as one of the best outdoor venues in Australia. This site has always made me really proud, and I look after it as if it were my second home — I landscaped it with ponds, waterfalls and bush tracks with the support of one of the landlords, Ray Hussey, who is an artist at the wheel of his diggers and loaders.

Being in the north of Australia the weather is great all year round and we're fortunate to be surrounded by some of the world's oldest rainforests. We even have barramundi breeding in the ponds and occasionally they find their way onto the barbeque. I've got a lot of special friends there and some of the best times I've ever had on a bungy site have happened while partying with friends and clients at our monthly full-moon parties. We operate the Minjin, a 40-metre jungle swing that races through the treetops, carrying up to three people at once. It's a real rush and the only one of its kind on the planet. We're planning to put in a bush flying fox and kids' adventure park next. We've also used the corporate-entertainment market to bolster the business's financial position really well, making the most of the great bar on the site and the scenic location. As good as it all looks in Cairns today, the upheaval of setting up the place and keeping it going is something I've found is pretty typical around the world.

In the early days the most tempting market to expand into was the United States. In the early nineties, bungy took off there big time. Too big. I was left with a dilemma — join the hordes rushing in or stand back and wait for the dust to settle. The litigation side of things in the US was very unclear, so we decided to wait on that market until the bubble burst.

It was highly predictable that with operators opening up overnight all over the place, a lot of them would stuff up, shut down and clear out. The other thing that was predictable was that these clowns would kill people, and I wanted no part of that. We'd seen these idiots trying to set up bungy sites in New Zealand, thinking it was an easy way to make a quick buck, until we'd got the New Zealand Standards put in place. That NZS system became pretty much the global standard. I'm proud of our efforts to promote it, because I know for a fact that it has saved lives by clearing out the dodgy operators.

So we waited. The US was an incredibly lucrative market but we didn't want to go in while it was in such a state of disarray and find ourselves involved in such a murky and dangerous atmosphere.

Shortly before bungy got banned in most of the states, there were about 350 different operators — no one knows the actual number for sure. Many of these people were just average Joes with access to a crane and a bit of rubber on the weekends. There was no serious standard Code of Practice and few of the operators were interested in setting and maintaining any sort of safety measures. If you could weasel your way to get insurance, then you could operate a bungy site. It was madness — anyone who fancied shoving paying punters off a crane tower at the weekends could set up a temporary site. Some of the safety practices were worrying at best and there were a couple of deaths in quick succession, one of which was caught on home video and broadcast on the television news across the country pretty much constantly.

Finally, one by one, the states banned bungy — and that's when we went in. Working with the authorities in Florida, where they had had a lot of problems, we helped them straighten out some of their issues and concerns. We also made it clear to them that bungy could be done safely. Gradually we eased open a regulated environment for bungy.

With the dodgy operators gone, we felt better about moving into this market with our top-end product and our excellent safety record. We even looked at buying into an outfit called Air Boingo, which was owned by a guy called Stan Checkers and his children. They used these little 20 metre towers and we gave some thought to setting up these things and using them as feeder sites to bigger towers within a couple of hours' drive. But the financial model didn't quite work out.

Eventually we opened a site in Las Vegas — a brilliant spot, visible from the main strip — and one in Florida. These spots brought bungy to a lot of people and made good revenue, proving that you can run a successful high-end product in such a hectic marketplace.

The Las Vegas site was the first one we had ever taken over that had been completely established by someone else. Originally, the tower was built as a viewing platform — for decades it was the tallest structure in Las Vegas. Two young Americans spotted the site and, with some useful connections on the local council (Las Vegas is still the kind of town where wheels need to be greased), they managed to get permission to turn the tower into a bungy site.

Sadly, they didn't know much about running a bungy business: one of their platforms jumped directly over tarmac and the other over the roof of their office. And they had little experience of marketing the product.

Within a couple of years the site was burdened with debt, but I was confident we could turn it around with the right management and the right incentives. So I took one of my best operators and closest friends, Mike Champoux, and gave him 30 per cent of the business on the proviso that he clear the debts and return the business to profitability. This was a smart deal, as Mike was a brilliant operator and this gave him just the motivation to drive the place to success. He was accountant, jump-master, marketing chief and dishwasher all wrapped up in one.

After a few years of Mike's efforts, the site was putting through 18,000 jumpers a year; a big rise on the 1,500 people the original operators managed in their first year. Mike got rid of all the debts, allowing us to purchase the property and for a while it was my most profitable site.

In 2005 we had an offer from a property developer to purchase the land under the tower. The offer was simply too good to refuse so, with some sadness, I closed one of my greatest bungy sites.

Next to Cairns, the Normandy bungy site — which also opened in 1990 — remains my favourite. I found this old rail viaduct designed by Gustave Eiffel, famous for a certain tower in Paris. The Viaduc de la Souleuvre, near Vire, two-and-a-half hours west of the French capital, had been abandoned since shortly after the Second World War. All that remained were the stout 60-metre high pillars that supported the original rail bridge. I was to spend months crawling around building a double suspension bridge and a jump platform. Every inch of the site took hours of labour, further cementing my connection to the business when we got it going. I got my old mate from home, Geoff Wilson, to fly over to help out, and we enlisted a couple of young Kiwi lads as labourers — Callum and Hamish, brothers from Timaru.

France was always going to be a good market for us. When we opened there the government had only just lifted a ban and legalised bungy again, and there were incredibly tight restrictions on what you could do and how it could be done, so it was a hard slog to win people around. Of course, being ignorant Kiwi boys, Henry and I didn't realise that Normandy could be so horrible and so miserable in the winter so we had a real hard time getting people out to the site. We naively thought that we could run a year-round operation, just like in Queenstown and Cairns, but in the winter, French people don't go anywhere near the coast. Pretty quickly we were forced to go from 365 operating days per year to 165, mostly over the summer. For eighteen months the site was open only at weekends, and then for just three months it would be open every day.

In building the site and in the first eight months of operation, Henry and I had poured NZ$800,000 into it. A major resurrection was needed. Jaque Gris was sent in there as general manager and his main role was to sack the entire 25-strong crew. Jaque's job as axeman took just one week, then we sent in Mike Champoux to head the recovery process. He rehired six staff on part-time contracts so that the business could stagger back into credibility.

We also had some pretty spectacular complications due to our lack of understanding of French law, especially employment law. In France, the workplace laws favour the employee, to a point where it makes it hellishly difficult to start up a small business. It was hard for us to take on casual staff for a seasonally affected operation because once we signed them on we were obliged to pay them, even when there was no work. This was a hell of an eye opener, coming from a background where good, honest Kiwis rolled up their sleeves, were flexible, realistic and did a good, honest day's work whenever it was available.

Our manager there, Christian Ferrier, did outstanding work in launching Le Scable — my first major venture outside of bungy jumping. Essentially it's a massive flying fox, which runs alongside the beautiful viaduct. As it developed I could see the potential we had for tapping into other adrenalin-based, gravity-defying activities. Right from the first day of watching Le Scable in action I knew that my business's future would not begin and end with the bits of rubber.

Of course, we've since come to terms with the labour laws in France and, it must be said, the Gallic attitudes to hard work have proved better than those in certain other places.

Welcome to sunny Acapulco! One of the most stunning bungy sites I've ever been involved with is right on a high-end stretch of beach in Mexico, the Condesa. From the top of the bungy tower you can see golden sand stretching around the 16 kilometre bay. The main highway brings travellers straight to the door and the pool beneath the bungy tower is right in the middle of a bunch of bars and restaurants. It's spectacular stuff and as it is right on the beach it get loads of foot traffic. Often hundreds of people, standing up to ten deep, watch the jumpers. Acapulco has become a big spring break destination, with loads of young Americans partying alongside the hardcore party crowd from Mexico City, making this one of the busiest bungy centres in the world.

Doing business in Mexico can be very draining for Westerners. As an outsider, it can be hard to get paid what you're due and to get things done when the local mañana factor is in effect. The local operator and I also diverge in our beliefs on the importance of safety, so after six years of being involved with this operation I've had to leave it behind. I'll still drop in there from time to time and help them out if I can, but it no longer trades as an AJ Hackett Bungy site. Would I like to return? Maybe mañana . . .

Bali has been another classic example of the clash between our Western safety standards and local operator practices. We set up at the 66 Club in Kuta Beach in March 1995 and within a couple of months there were other tower operators and one crane operator within a few square kilometres of each other. They didn't realise that the market is fairly finite, so in fact they split the market, meaning all these sites underperformed.

We had tried some crane jumps through Britain and Ireland in the early 1990s and had a great time doing it, but the operating costs were too high. We get a lot of gap year travellers at our sites, young Britons seeing the world before committing to a career. Possibly because so many of them go seeking adventure like this, they make great bungy customers. Interestingly, the Irish are possibly the worst for freezing on the jump platform and pulling out at the last minute. And there always seemed something a bit tacky about those other temporary set-ups.

I think a lot of our customers felt the same way about these other sites in Bali. One of those other operators killed two customers on a swing from their bungy tower, making things even tougher for all in the local bungy trade.

We dug in our heels with Bali and shouldered a lot of expenses, like in Acapulco. But, like in Acapulco, our local partner — a powerful local businessman called Kadek — had some issues. Again, the necessity for us to impose Western standards of safety and operating practices was a major problem. It took a lot of time, and plenty of tense meetings — at one point, we withdrew totally from the business, as I've now done in Acapulco. Eventually, the Bali site became so run-down that it was relatively easy to convince Kadek that he had to either invest a truckload, close it down for fear of killing someone, or let me come back in to run the business myself. He let me back in.

I wanted to help Kadek. Just before I went back into running the site in 2003, a bomb went off at a bar he owned in town called Paddy's. As survivors ran from the building into the street, a van loaded with more explosives erupted into flames. Hundreds died in the street. Among the victims were many Australians, for whom Bali was a popular holiday destination. It was a terrible tragedy and a vile criminal act.

These were dark days for Bali, whose economy is heavily reliant on tourism. The island's reputation and perseverance was just starting to see it right, when sickening violence struck again. Almost two years to the day, there was a second bomb attack, and this time it was almost a killer blow for the tourism industry. Today Bali is seriously struggling to get back on its feet due in no small part to what are, in my view, some tactless, scaremongering politics from the Australian Prime Minister John Howard. His government has kept travel warnings in place when other Western nations have lifted theirs. The Aussie press hasn't helped with ridiculous amounts of publicity heaped upon minor drug busts involving Australians in Bali.

I'm sure if a bomb were to go off in Sydney, the Australian Government would not want the rest of the world to dump a crippling travel warning on their country for an unnecessary amount of time. I find Bali one of the safest and most pleasant places to visit on the planet. AJ Hackett International is committed for the long run there, regardless of what terrorist idiots or reactionary Western politicians throw at the place next.

Perhaps the oddest international extension of bungy came when my old mate Chris Allum convinced the organisers of the X-Games to include it in their repertoire of events. Chris — 'the Doctor' — had been operating a bungy site attached to a bar on the waterfront in New York for some years. Hanging in there during the wild days when the dodgy operators cleared out of the industry, the Doctor had made a name for himself as a reliable operator. He recalls a balloon operator who used to do commercial jumps from two heights: 50 metres and 100 metres. Predictably, one paying customer was given the 100 metre cord when jumping from 50 metres. It's a pretty simple equation.

But the Doctor had a good reputation, and when bungy was lined up to appear at the X Games he was adamant that the operational standard to be used would be the one we developed in New Zealand. He cut a deal to have a bunch of his old mates from Queenstown flown in to run things at the Rhode Island event. Adam Lichtenstein was a jump-master, along with Hippy and Kevin Jennings, a Yank who was one of the Kawarau Bridge originals. Naturally, I was a celebrity judge, sitting at ground level, giving the final say on whether or not the jumpers had made the grade.

So all of a sudden, these 'X-athletes' were somersaulting and vaulting about the place as part of some bizarre spectacular in front of a stadium full of teenage American skateboarders. The jumpers dived from a purpose-built 50 metre tower and some of them had never bungied before, while others had experience as competitive high divers.

It was great to get together with a heap of guys I wasn't seeing so much of any more. There were old friends, now running other bungy companies, that we were supposed to be competing against, but of course we all got on like a house on fire. We found time in the evenings to have a few drinks, and along the way we befriended a guy who was involved in running the X Games. He was called Vinnie and he was something of a local wise guy — a connected man. He approached me one day while I was judging at the bungy and he said: 'Why are you sitting on those chairs? I've got a friend who owes me a favour.' Within a couple of hours, these great big leather chairs were delivered and the guys and I sat there like the kings of the world. 'Anytime you need anything, just call me,' says Vinnie. 'And I mean anything,' he said with a raised eyebrow. Well, all we could ever think of to call him for was more beer when we ran out at the end of each night. Although there was one night when even Vinnie's beer ran out and I tried to book a helicopter to fly us to Manhattan.

The high-diver guys in the competition pretty much took it out every time. They'd be doing multiple tucks and turns, flips, somersaults and reverse dives that we, the professionals, had never thought of. Then some chubby Japanese BMX rider would get up there and do a bellyflop.

Bungy is really too predictable for that sort of event. Too precise. People were expecting a bit of carnage and bungy didn't fit that model — not the way we ran it. There was the discipline part, which was like watching the high dive at the Olympics, which is fine and good but it wasn't actually all that radical compared with people face planting off BMXs or skateboards. Of course there was no way we could have people face plant from a 50-metre bungy tower. So bungy was only part of the X-Games for two years, at which point I guess the organisers realised we weren't going to face plant anyone and we stopped getting invited. It sure was a fun junket while it lasted.

Growing the international side of the business has always been my priority. The challenge of working in new environments and dealing with people from different cultures is rewarding for me, and that's why I never based myself permanently in Queenstown. Once the operation there was under way, I headed off to live in France where I raised my family.

From Mexico, through Macau and into Cairns, I've learnt that the only way to do business across a wide variety of cultures is to build long-term trust. You have a blue and you work it out. In the case of Bali, we backed out of the business altogether for a while when we had differences with the local operator about which way things should go. Even during that period, I was flying in there and making sure everything at the site was running well. Still maintaining that relationship of trust.

My take from the international businesses is usually about ten per cent. Which is quite a lot if you're a local operator and that's going straight off the top of your company's turnover. Of course, in cases where I own the company or have shares in it, I'm getting my take there as well as the ten per cent. My partners also have to put up with me arriving on the site several times a year and pestering management and owners about things in order to keep up the standards and foster constant change.

AJ Hackett International has outlasted all the serious competition. There are a couple of very professional operators in Switzerland and Germany, and every now and again someone sees a quick buck can be made from a crane doing a few inaccurate jumps. They never last — they never really set out to last. They want to make what they see as a bit of easy money, then they clear out. Thank God.

Today, AJ Hackett Bungy sites have had more than two million jumps globally — God, I was feeling old when we hit one million, back in the late nineties. That's two million people taking a life-changing experience courtesy of my bits of rubber. Who would have thought?!

CHAPTER 9

Sharpening
up our game

Maybe we had it too good for too long. It was always going to be interesting to see how we would fare when someone tried to take us on directly in our own markets. After four years of steady business in Queenstown and with the international side of things becoming quite hectic, word got to me that competition was really coming home to roost. The company that ran the scenic gondola in Queenstown was planning to set up a bungy operation right in the heart of the town. The Ledge, as it is called today, was to be a small jump, but the spot was incredibly scenic, with great views over Queenstown, the Remarkables and Lake Wakatipu, and its convenience was a massive drawcard for customers. Whereas the Kawarau Bridge was a fifteen-minute drive from the town and our other much higher site at Skippers Canyon was about an hour's drive, this site would be a short walk from the lakefront bars and shops.

Internationally, there were plenty of other bungy operators getting a cut of the pie we had baked. Mostly they weren't really competition for us as none of them were serious about establishing long-term sites. Generally, they were operating from crane towers. There were a lot of these mobile bungy operators popping up around New Zealand too. The east coast beaches on the North Island sprouted cranes every summer and Taupo Bungy had been running a very successful set up in the central North Island since 1991. But until the Ledge came along, no one had successfully brought a bungy into our backyard.

By 1993, other forms of competition had sprouted up around Queenstown since we had kick-started the region's adventure-tourism market. These operators were generally complementary to us. If visitors came to Queenstown for the mountain biking or the parapenting, then we could probably get them to spend money on bungy while they were in town. But this Ledge bungy set-up would be different: a bungy competitor right on our doorstep. We had to take a look at ourselves and figure out how we could become sharper; what we could do to meet the threat of competition. We needed to cut costs to absorb the anticipated losses as the market became diluted and we needed to make ourselves a better operation with a better product.

It was obvious to me that the Ledge operation would be only the first of what could amount to many other serious domestic competitors for the Queenstown market. I wanted to take positive steps, rather than stand around waiting for the flood of competition to come and the wolf to be at the door — we had to be ready and lean for the fight. We had to tighten up at Kawarau and Skippers. The Skyline Gondola was then — and remains today — the busiest destination in Queenstown, so as a location for a bungy site it had an awful lot going for it. Pretty much everyone who visits Queenstown goes up the gondola, has lunch, takes in the views, then comes down — so your market's right there.

We were doing a lot of stuff overseas, working on sites that were hard to develop and facing some rough competition and a huge learning curve in international business. Meanwhile, Queenstown had become this massive, fat, cash-generating and cash-consuming cow, but it was consuming far too much. A culture of corporate excess was already starting to develop there. Other sites in the group elsewhere around the world were struggling to grow, occasionally having trouble paying the wage bills, and yet in Queenstown the staff were driving around in flash new four wheel drive vehicles and everyone seemed to have their own offices in a building opposite the shiny new bungy centre, The Station. I wanted to milk the beast to feed and ensure the survival of the developing businesses, while it seemed that everyone based in Queenstown was happy to simply enjoy the ride on the beast without any commitment to our international interests.

I planned some drastic action. Andy Brinsley was our general manager and, as my partner on the ground, Henry was well placed to know what was going on. But the company bore my name and I was determined to sharpen it up. It was clear that I needed to come in over the heads of both of them. Being based in France gave me an advantage — I wasn't involved in the day-to-day management in Queenstown and could see the problem more clearly than the guys on the ground.

With the news of the Ledge site ringing in my ears, I flew in to Queenstown and called a crisis meeting with Andy and Henry. 'Look fellas, in three months' time when these guys open, we need to be lean. If we lose 20 per cent of our jumps, we've had it. We will be screwed because this place has become so expensive to run, and things are already extremely tight overseas.'

Henry could see where I was coming from but Andy was not convinced. I think Henry recognised that we had become this large corporate entity that required a massive, constant customer flow to sustain it. We had to take action there and then, or we would be knocked hard by the effect of this new competition, even if they only took a small slice of our business. What I proposed was fairly much a clearing out of middle management staff. I showed Andy and Henry a list of names of staff, many of whom were friends of ours. Andy was great with people and fantastic for our operation, but I told him: 'Mate, we've got so many people here that we don't need. I'm lining up for war. Some people simply have to go.'

He hated it. 'AJ, we've got a good business model working here. For three years we've been producing great results with a stable crew. It turns out we're pretty good at running a successful bungy business. If costs need to be checked and brought into line, then we can find ways to do that. We don't need to sack people.'

Andy felt at the time — and still does now — that I was being pretty unreasonable: coming in from afar and dictating terms. He felt that I was in thrall to management consultants who saw nothing but fat to be cut and advocated change for change's sake. It's true, right from the early days, I had been bringing in people as consultants and motivational speakers and I know some of the guys thought it was naff, but for plenty of the others it worked really well. And I loved to hear what outsiders had to say about our business and to learn from their ideas on how we could improve.

As Andy saw it, the business was ticking over nicely and there was no need to rock the boat. The discussions were heated, but my mind was made up. I made a dozen staff redundant on that trip — about 25 per cent of our workforce.

Andy was livid. 'I had to sit through seeing some good people get booted out,' he says. 'And they were people I knew well. We socialised together and they were sound at their jobs, so to see them getting run out was painful. It changed the culture within the company too. The whole experience left a nasty aftertaste.'

It was the first time in the life of our Queenstown business that we'd been forced to take such brutal action and it didn't feel good for anyone. All of a sudden I went from being this cheerful, hopefully inspirational, figurehead for the business — the guy who flew in from France once in a while to party and bungy — to being the big bad employer. The guy who sacks your mates — just another fascist boss. I hated doing it but felt at the time — and still feel today — that we had to do something to get ready for the competition that was on the way.

In bringing about those redundancies, my actions flushed the real competition out of the woodwork in a way I could never have imagined.

A couple of weeks after that stressful trip and the heated meetings, Andy and our international operations manager, Glenn Russell (Hippy), announced that they were leaving to set themselves up as Bungy Consultants New Zealand Ltd. So our general manager and our operations manager walked out the door. Henry was devastated and saw their departure as a personal insult — he

filled the breach left by Andy, taking over as general manager
and keeping the ball rolling at Kawarau Bridge and at Skippers
Canyon. A few weeks after they departed, the news was even
worse: they weren't simply going to be bungy consultants, they
were opening a new site right in Queenstown. Their new bungy
jump at the Pipeline gorge would be bigger than either of our
sites and it would be handier to town than Skippers Canyon, our
highest site. The Ledge jump by the gondola was still going to
come — but the big bungy battle would be between Pipeline and
us. And it had a personal touch: two of my best mates had walked
out of my business with all the know-how Henry and I had instilled
in them and were setting up as our opposition.

When Hippy and Andy set up, their site would be the highest
— 102 metres, and along with the loss of their expertise, they
also stole a couple of our best jump-masters — Tim Sykes and
Stu Karina. The Pipeline broke the magic 100 metre barrier,
establishing a template in Queenstown bungy that pretty much
remains true today — you either jump the original, or you jump
the tallest. The Pipeline was the same price as the Skippers jump,
but 30 metres higher and closer to town, so overnight the market
for Skippers just died. Young travellers are always looking to get
value for money and Pipeline nailed us on that one.

I'd be lying if I said I was delighted that my general manager
and my operations manager had buggered off to become our
main rivals, but a big part of me was quietly proud of them and
full of admiration. The spirit they had and the gumption they
displayed were reminiscent of what Henry and I had done at the
Kawarau Bridge when we kicked off there back in the 1980s.

I reckon Hippy was always going to leave to set up Pipeline,
but it was a shock when Andy went as well. To lose two fantastic

operators — never mind the fact that they were dynamite blokes and top mates of mine — was a real blow. In particular, I was really sad that Andy left. Without Andy in Pipeline, their set-up may not have had the same impact upon us — he had such good ideas for running and promoting a streamlined business. But Hippy is a top operations manager anyway and, of course, there was that magic 100-metre mark.

I wasn't angry with them at all — I respected that they had the balls to go and I felt flattered that we'd started something that they felt inspired enough to continue with. For Henry, their departure seemed a more personal blow and I don't know if he ever really forgave them.

This was a hell of a tough time for Henry. He was back in the office running the business from Kawarau, filling the breach left by Andy Brinsley. It was hard to admit defeat at Skippers, so we kept the site going for another two or three years, but overnight it had gone from 15,000 jumps a year to 5,000 a year. Skippers was leaking money horrendously. We had a garage with three full-time mechanics just to look after the vehicles we needed to ferry customers up to the Skippers bungy site — ours was the biggest private fleet of Land Rovers in the country. What a nightmare. All these vehicles on account of a business set-up that was stuffed and losing loads of money.

Over at Pipeline, things were done in a more simple way and fun was a central component. There was a guerilla ethos that made the Pipeline seem an enjoyable project to work on. They had to do a little trickery to get past the resource consents procedure. You weren't allowed to build a new bridge for a bungy platform, so Andy and Hippy 'restored an existing structure' — an old bridge supporting a pipeline — and the minute it was restored, they put in an application to run bungy jumps off an existing structure. Doing this meant that they got the whole platform set up and built without having to do any public notifications — ingenious.

Suddenly bungy was exciting again. It was like the early days at Kawarau Bridge with a really wild adventurous spirit and feeling to it. When Pipeline opened, they didn't have any brochures or pictures of it around town, so all the initial buzz spread through Queenstown by word of mouth. It was back to basics. All the local tourism outlets knew Andy and Hippy were sound operators, so they knew they could trust them and recommend them without fear of sending tourists to their deaths. While we were running a fleet of vehicles and selling everything from espresso to hooded sweatshirts, the Pipeline boys contracted out the transport to someone else and stuck to their core activity, which was the biggest bungy jump in New Zealand.

Hippy remembers how the culture at Pipeline was reminiscent of the first days of bungy in Queenstown. 'The personal touch was always important in the early days at the Kawarau Bridge. By the time you walked out on to the bridge with the customer you knew who they were, where they were from, what they did for a job and where they were going to be drinking that night. I think that had been lost a bit at Kawarau as the scale had grown and, for a while at least, we managed to keep it alive at Pipeline.'

The fact that Pipeline was like the early days of the Kawarau Bridge vindicated my concerns about the regimented corporate environment we had become. Although it's nice to milk a monopoly, it just makes you bloated in the long run.

As much as Andy complained bitterly about me cutting our staffing levels back when he was managing things for AJ Hackett Bungy, he always ran a very tight ship at the Pipeline and has continued to do so in all his business dealings since. I like to think that he learnt something valuable from me: he saw that it's best to keep your business lean and tight from the start so that you don't have to let people go.

As they developed and their business grew, the marketing at Pipeline was a lot different from ours, which had become very corporate. They were looser and kept relying on that word-of-mouth factor. It's galling to admit but, for a while there, it was actually really cool to jump the Pipeline, as opposed to jumping at AJ Hackett. This is a great example of the stronger brand not necessarily being the biggest deal.

There were some funny scenes when staff from the AJ Hackett Bungy site would bump into the Pipeline boys in town having a few beers after a long day. At first, we would regard one another warily across the bar in Eichardt's, but before long we would all be drinking together — after all, we were old mates. Now, of course, we would lie about how many jumps we had sold that day and try to pry for trade secrets.

Pipeline had a great motto that summed up the original spirit of the bungy trade: 'If you're living on the edge, you're taking up too much room.' Most customers thinking about trying a bungy will think of AJ Hackett first, so there was a lot of interest in how the Pipeline boys would go against our bigger, stronger brand. The willingness of so many punters to go for the Pipeline in such numbers suggested to me that the new site was tapping into the original spirit of bungy. They had an edge, and in order to compete with them, we would need to find one too.

The Pipeline guys still had shares in the AJ Hackett Group from when we all bought out the Cairns site. They had to get rid of their shares because they were now competitors — typically they didn't miss a chance to rub our noses in it.

'On pretty much the first day of operating at the Pipeline, the AJ Hackett accountant came to see us so we could sign the papers ending our involvement with them,' says Andy. 'We were just chocka. Vehicles were pouring up the hill and people were clamouring to jump the Pipeline. Of course we made the accountant wait and watch and we made a terrific show of how busy we were. Eventually, we deigned to sign the papers, right there on the side of the bridge — and then we were free. It felt fantastic.'

With Pipeline's arrival, the Skippers' jump was now a sink into which running costs would steadily trickle, and we felt Pipeline's presence at the Kawarau Bridge too. We even noticed it across the Tasman in Cairns. A year or two after Pipeline was established, we estimated that the Australian site had been losing about 5,000 jumps a year to them. There had always been an element of competition between our site in Cairns and our site in Queenstown: someone travelling through northeast Australia might reasonably figure that they would wait until they were in New Zealand, the mecca of bungy jumping, before signing on for a leap. But the Pipeline effect showed it most starkly, and these were customers that we were losing not to one of our own sites, but to a rival operator. Lately the Cairns site has had to deal with a rise in other activities which have blossomed in the past decade. In the last few years tandem skydiving has become huge in the area.

Pipeline had trumped us for height — they had the edge — but the solution was obvious. We would have to seize the initiative by going one better and trumping them right back. Henry had a higher trump card. He had long been looking out for new sites to develop and the best one he settled on was at the Nevis River, which runs down into the Kawarau Gorge. It took a couple of years to open a site at the Nevis that would be even taller than the Pipeline. It was a special jump site. A $2 million jump pod ferries customers out to a platform suspended by cables 134 metres above the Nevis River. Once that site opened it effectively knocked the Pipeline operation out of the game. It was all Henry's work, beautifully conceived and ambitiously executed. The Nevis killed off demand for the Pipeline, just as the Pipeline had killed off Skippers.

By the time the Nevis was launched, Andy and Hippy had already sold up their share of the Pipeline with Ngai Tahu, the big South Island Maori tribe, taking over along with the landowner. The tribe was left with a bit of a lemon and a few years later when the Nevis started up, Henry bought the Pipeline operation for a song, giving some nice breadth to the AJ Hackett Bungy operations in Queenstown. And, wouldn't you know it, a decade after they had us tearing out our hair, Andy and Hippy are stirring things up again by trying to get council consent for an even higher jump site just outside Queenstown.

I still believe that having Andy and Hippy start Pipeline was a good thing for our business. It shook us out of this corporate shell we were in by snaffling a decent chunk of our market — as many as 15,000 jumps a year had gone. Boom. It hurt like hell at the time, but it made us sharpen our game.

Oh, and the Ledge, the sweet little 30-metre leap that had triggered the whole drama, had also landed in the AJ Hackett Bungy portfolio by then. By outlasting our competitors and being bold enough to absorb them when the opportunities arose, we had reclaimed the high ground.

Over the years we've crossed swords with other operators internationally, but nothing tested us — and ultimately improved us — as much as the challenge from Pipeline. We found most of our competitors in the United States based their businesses on a fast turn-around of clients and a quick training time for staff — one had this little school they put people through and at the end of a three-week programme you were suddenly a jump-master. Our competitors had a cheap, fast-food approach to the business compared with what I liked to think was a consummate feast at AJ Hackett Bungy. They liked to boast that their systems were virtually idiot proof — usually this is right about the time that you employ someone who is beyond idiocy and the whole thing goes wrong with a splat.

I would hate to fast track the training of a jump-master. It's like driving a car: after a week or so, you have probably figured out enough to get behind the wheel and you might stall occasionally or graunch the gears, but your passengers are generally going to be better off — and safer — with an experienced set of hands in control.

Operating in the high end of the business meant that we had greater costs and took on more debt, but it also meant we always had a stronger market position than our competitors, giving us the ability to persevere.

CHAPTER 10

Carving up the
golden chook

Henry van Asch and I had been mates for a decade. We had travelled the world together, setting up our unique business, surviving the hassles of rapid growth and hectic competition, and we'd had a pretty bloody good time along the way. We had created an industry in which we could employ our mates, party like it was going out of fashion and jump off extremely tall things all over the globe. Superb fun.

We met through skiing in Wanaka in 1985 and hit it off straight away, sharing a similar taste for madness, adrenalin and adventure. Henry was really enthusiastic about speed skiing; he'd busted a gut to get the best gear possible and had really cranked out some impressive times. As a skier he was aggressive, attacking the snow and working really hard to burn through runs — there were never any easy turns and gentle slopes with Henry, it was full throttle all the way.

He was the driving force behind a bunch of us going on the European ski tour in 1987. When he put his mind to something he was intense, driven and overtly ambitious. Aside from the skiing, where he set national records, Henry also became an excellent mountain biker and was largely responsible for the rapid growth of this sport in New Zealand. We both shared a focused desire to drive determinedly for a goal, even though our styles were completely different in achieving the same objective.

By 1997, underlying tensions in our relationship were surfacing more and more. The way we both looked at our business differed greatly: my focus by this point was almost entirely on the international side of the set-up, while Henry lived in Queenstown and concentrated more on the operations there. It seemed to me that he viewed the Queenstown hub as the pinnacle of what we were about, whereas I saw it as a launching pad.

There were also major differences in our personalities. I'm a pretty easy-going kind of guy — when I arrive at one of our bungy sites, the first thing I'll do is go and have a beer with some of the crew and catch up with a couple of old friends. I like to wander around and get a feel for the place. When I've flown in from halfway around the world, the last thing I want is to get tied down in meeting the management. Henry's style is somewhat different — he's more likely to want to get down to business as soon as the hellos are out of the way. He'll want to sit down with the site manager and go over the figures. Henry would be asking why the jump numbers were down compared with the previous month and what was being done to boost visitor numbers at about the same time that I'd be asking if there was another beer in the fridge. Over a couple of drinks, the staff will give me the real low-down on what's happening.

Our differing styles complemented each other nicely for a long time as the business was growing. Henry would drive things through and demand the best from all of the staff, while I'd perhaps be shaking hands with the crew, the clients and the press before going over the hard numbers with the manager. Later, when the business was sorted out, Henry would loosen up. Once the books were checked and the figures thoroughly gone over, Henry would unwind with the staff. Personally, I've always felt better getting my unwinding out of the way before any winding up could begin.

When staff left a meeting with Henry, they could generally expect a pretty lengthy list of detailed instructions arising from the meeting. They could also expect to be hounded as to what they were doing to keep up with the instructions or why they hadn't already carried out the instructions. Henry makes himself clear about what he wants. He expects a lot — and, mostly as a result of expecting it and demanding it, he gets it. Conversely, my style was always to put faith in the staff we had hired and back them to figure out the best way to do their jobs.

Perhaps the key to our differences was in the way we dealt with people; how we managed our staff and addressed clients, stakeholders, suppliers, the press and business partners. Our approaches differed in terms of sticks and carrots. I never wanted to motivate by fear and Henry probably felt I was too laid-back. This made it tough for the people working alongside us. A staff member who worked directly for both of us told me: 'Working for these two guys with such contrasting styles and temperaments was nigh on impossible. The way you'd answer to one and deal with the other were completely different.' This actually sounds an awful lot like the way I used to have to deal with my parents when I was a kid.

I felt that Henry was too abrupt with people — not with me of course, as we were old mates and business partners. But there were times when he was really foul to some people — staff or other people in the industry generally — and I would find myself backing him up because he was my business partner, although I didn't like it. Even in the most tense commercial haggling, you still have to keep your fundamental decency.

There were other issues too, of course. The fact that I lived in France, had a wife and two kids and was always travelling between international sites meant I wasn't always easily contactable when the man from the bank came knocking or when important decisions needed to be made. Henry often felt that he was at the coalface of the Queenstown operation while I was drifting in parts unknown. It would be easy to imagine that I was leading the lazy life in some French villa while Henry did the hard yards in New Zealand — and I'm the first to admit that I can be very difficult to contact. I was a latecomer to the mobile telephone revolution and tended to go off the radar for days at a time when I was at any of the sites as I give that site a hundred per cent of my attention for the whole time I'm there.

The fundamental difference between Henry and myself came down to the way we felt the company should develop. Yes, we had a fantastic product in Cairns and Queenstown, and yes, they had developed very quickly into reliable profit centres. Once we had seen off the competition, the Kawarau Bridge bungy site ticked over nicely and in a pretty short space of time our business had become part of the scenery. A Queenstown institution.

But it was never in my nature to rest on my laurels — I was relentless about pushing into new markets, growing our business and not just milking it. I expended most of my time and energy flying around the globe between the developing sites — from Bali, through Cairns, up to Las Vegas and back via Normandy — I was always on the go. I felt a responsibility on behalf of the overseas sites to keep them funded properly, and when these sites were being built — especially the Normandy one — I was drawing on the financial resources of the AJ Hackett Bungy operations in Australasia.

I tend to focus completely on a job when I'm immersed in it and building the Normandy site was no exception, so I probably seemed a bit curt and demanding at times when it came to getting money from the sites in New Zealand and Australia for our other projects. I know it used to bug our old general managers Andy Brinsley and Evan Bloomfield when they would get a fax saying: 'Please send 40 grand now, love AJ.' I imagine Henry would have found it exasperating as well.

Likewise, I was irritated that staff in New Zealand were driving around in brand new vehicles and wasting money on what seemed like luxuries to me, when sometimes we couldn't even pay a couple of grand for the wages at other sites that were having a harder time of it. That was ultimately what made me feel distant from the culture in Queenstown.

Henry's treatment of people had not improved. In my opinion, he was getting worse, leading a hectic single-man's lifestyle and habitually making what I felt were unreasonable demands of people.

For these reasons and many more, after ten great years together Henry and I had become like a couple in the middle of a marriage crisis. Our fundamental differences were exposed, the strengths that we each brought to the relationship had been surpassed by our feelings towards one another's weaknesses. We bickered. In short, the magic was gone.

I arrived in Queenstown for a three month stint, with Caroline and our sons, Dean and Jayde, in tow. Things with Henry were at an impasse, so I confronted him at a tense meeting and told him I wanted him to take time out, and leave me in charge of things for a while. He wanted to stay on, so I said I couldn't continue as we were and we would have to split the business. The realisation that we had to go our separate ways hit hard. I was shattered. One week into my three month stint in Queenstown, I was flying back to France, saddened by the extent of my falling out with an old and dear friend. We got Coopers and Lybrand to value the company and settled in to negotiate. It was time to divorce.

There has been an awful lot of speculation over the years about what went on in the negotiations between Henry and me at the time of our divorce. I would have loved to have kept the business intact and entirely in my possession, and I'm sure Henry would have loved to have it all in his possession too. We sat down to a series of protracted and often heated meetings to decide how to go our separate ways.

Ultimately, I wanted a resolution that would quickly put us both in a position to get on with addressing the real issues the operation needed to face to ensure the ongoing survival of our bungy sites. When we decided to split, I figured that the Queenstown operation should go to Henry as he was settled and happy living in the area.

Likewise, it seemed natural that the overseas operations should be controlled and owned by me, as I had shown them the most attention and was based in France. This was a fair split. With all negotiations, I find the best way to see if the deal you are offering is fair is to offer the reverse. I told Henry that, if he wanted, I would happily take the Queenstown operation and he could have the international side.

It would be painful to give up Queenstown. During our series of meetings in Auckland, it became increasingly clear that not only did Henry want Queenstown, he also wanted the lion's share of AJ Hackett Bungy. The doggedness that had served him so well as a competitive athlete and as part owner of a growing enterprise in the tough tourism sector was brought to bear in our negotiations. Henry liked where he was in the business, there's a certain status attached to being at the top of a successful operation like ours and, frankly (despite the stress and the hassles), it's fun.

Friends like Andy Brinsley and Hippy travelled up to Auckland to support me. Staff from throughout the organisation implored me to hang in there with the negotiations. This was a rough time for our employees — everyone seemed to feel that they had to take a side in this developing feud between the two big bosses and the uncertainty about the future direction of the global operation was painfully destabilising. Henry and I had a lot at stake in the divorce — I had a family to think of, but there were also more than 100 staff members around the world whose livelihood depended on us managing the split properly.

Queenstown, of course, is the goose that lays the golden egg. You couldn't invent a better bungy site than the Kawarau Bridge — a fifteen-minute drive from the region's major tourist hub, surrounded by beautiful mountains with a rustic old bridge to which we had secured relatively easy access from day one. At the time of our separation, AJ Hackett Bungy had a 60 year operating licence from the Department of Conservation on the bridge itself.

And it has tourists. Oh boy, does it have tourists, rolling out there by the busload every day. More tourists than you can shake a stick at. About six per cent of all visitors to Queenstown will jump at the Kawarau Bridge. That's 30-odd-thousand jumpers a year and the best reputation in the world of adventure sports — managed properly, the site would be a healthy, long-term goldmine. In short, if you run the Queenstown operation properly, you will never go hungry. Naturally, we would both see how strong an asset Queenstown was.

But Henry wanted more: he wanted Cairns. Henry wanted a split in the business that would have seen him take the New Zealand and Australian operations while I took everything else. 'Everything else' in this context meaning a series of basket-case bungy sites, variously in debt, understaffed or poorly resourced. There was Las Vegas and Normandy. At the time Vegas had a half-million dollar debt and some serious management issues, while Normandy was making a little money but was operating only seasonally. The Bali site was an issue in itself — we just weren't getting paid our royalties out of there. To be cast adrift with that lot and nothing else would mean sinking pretty quickly.

I also wanted more — to be paid out for parting with Queenstown and to get a royalty from the operation there.

The divorce negotiations were a protracted affair, lasting several months and ageing me by several years. Henry and I would meet in hotels or offices surrounded by lawyers, accountants or business advisers. Sometimes we managed to get through the meetings in a cordial fashion, but often there was shouting and name calling. We both stormed out more than once. It was tense and I saw an ugly, hard-bitten side to my former business partner more than once.

Once we had settled the details of the physical split — who got which sites in which countries — the last remaining sticking point was the question of intellectual property rights. Henry wanted a contract saying that the brand, which was to be jointly owned by us, was AJ Hackett. For me this was out of the question; the brand was AJ Hackett Bungy. If he owned the brand 'AJ Hackett' then Henry could put my name on anything. We were both tenacious, but in the end the brand was settled as 'AJ Hackett Bungy'. We signed our divorce papers and got on with our futures.

After we settled, I met Andy Brinsley and Hippy for a beer.

'That's it, fellas,' I told them. 'It's all over.'

'How did you split it?'

'Henry gets New Zealand and I get . . . a world full of opportunities!'

'A world full of hassles you mean!'

They implored me to hang in there.

'Henry came into bungy with nothing and now you've given him everything, AJ!'

'This is your business, AJ! It's got your name on it for crying out loud! You invented this thing and Queenstown is the biggest part of the deal. You can't just walk away!'

They were wrong. I could walk and I did. I knew that with the Cairns operation in my side of the divide there was a great chance to rebuild my bungy business from the ground up. At the end of the day you have to cut your losses and move on — the divorce had battered me, but I was determined to see the positives. Henry was seriously focused on New Zealand and everything outside the country would be controlled by me. He had great staff and, if he wanted to, could just sit at the Kawarau Bridge and watch the cash roll in. The riskier option — the more exciting and challenging path — was taking the international side of the divorce settlement. And hadn't I gotten into bungy in the first place for the challenge and excitement?

Other than Cairns, which by now was a very solid business, I knew I would have my hands full massaging the various sites around the planet into something approaching a viable business. But I was willing to sustain a lot of hassles with the international sites as I had incredibly loyal, focused teams who were absolutely committed to their success. I'm interested in different cultures and different ways that people operate so I was determined to make my side of this divorce work. The way I see things, I don't care about the details of hassles: I'll sort them out as they arise, because I know that long term my bungy jumping concept will come through.

So Henry got the golden chook and I got all the damaged ducklings. The deal we cut saw him take the Queenstown business. Normally when someone gets a licence agreement with me to use my name and my bungy system, I get a standard 10 per cent of the income at the site. Here I took nothing. I walked away from the destructive discussions with no slice of New Zealand. When people jump at the AJ Hackett Bungy at Kawarau Bridge not one red cent goes into AJ Hackett's pocket.

The split wasn't 100 per cent clean. After the divorce, Henry and I still shared a pre-existing stake in the Bali site. But Henry was never all that interested in it and Kadek, the local partner in

Bali who owned the site, had never liked to deal with Henry so eventually I took the management of that one. Henry and I also kept a shared interest in a film company that some friends ran in New Zealand but we soon turned that stake over to the couple who ran the company, so that was pretty much our last shared interest.

And there's the name: AJ Hackett. That's me.

After the divorce, Henry gave some thought to changing the name of the business in New Zealand. There was nothing stopping him from changing the name — from the moment the Queenstown operation became his business Henry could have called it van Asch Bungy. I know it must be galling for Henry to run a business with my name on it. Many customers out at the Kawarau Bridge still expect to see AJ Hackett carrying the ropes around the place and running the whole show. The staff are Henry's, yet their uniforms have my name on them. I suspect Henry knows as well as I do that to change the name of the business would be a bad move. The 100 per cent safety record is built around my name and the systems and practices that we developed.

Despite the fact that I was no longer directly involved, he kept my name on his business, which was fine by me. I know that Henry will always run a top-notch bungy outfit and — direct involvement or not, share of the profits or not — I'm proud for my name to be associated with his operation in Queenstown. We also still have tie-ins, where the interest of my global group match his interest in New Zealand. My marketing on the international side sometimes dovetails with Henry's marketing in New Zealand. On operational stuff we are very closely connected — if someone finds a better way of doing something or a safer method of transporting a bungy cord, then we make sure that everyone at all our sites knows. We still sing from the same songbook on operational matters and still work with the same safety standards. A lot of staff cross over from Henry's sites to mine and back again. Today Henry has some new partners in the business.

Bungy is one of those nice products where once you get the volume happening, the market will keep flowing. As long as Henry keeps running a tidy operation in Queenstown, it'll all tick over nicely for him. One of Henry's strengths is his organisational skills and getting a good team under him at management level. He's got a nice business there in Queenstown, and they've tried out an interesting development with their move into the Auckland market for the Harbour Bridge walk and bungy. Henry has opened a great restaurant right by the Kawarau site and he's also started his own vineyard, so he's got interests outside of the rubber cord game. He lives with his wife Caroline and three great kids in a beautiful house near Queenstown and, with me not around, he's pretty much the bungy-man-about-town. He likes to be acknowledged as the co-founder of bungy jumping — there's some mana that comes with that, so that's nice for him.

The tourism market has been a bit soft in New Zealand for a couple of years now, as the dollar has gotten stronger. The sterling doesn't go anywhere near as far as it used to, but Henry and the Queenstown crew are in a really strong position, and have been able to weather the tough times pretty well.

At the end of the day, everything has turned out all right. Henry and I have got a few more wrinkles and bruises than when we started, for sure, but in the big picture, we've both done pretty damn well out of bungy and our business relationship.

CHAPTER 11

The ultimate adrenalin rush

There's nothing like a homecoming. On 5 October 1998
I stood on a platform 192 metres above the concrete pavements of
Auckland City. Cameras flashed in the darkness from the crowd
gathered around the base of the Sky Tower. From where I stood,
I could see across the harbour to the lights of the North Shore
suburbs where I grew up — and almost as far as the Greenhithe
Bridge, where my career in bungy began. I could see the Stock
Exchange building where I did my first highly publicised jump
in New Zealand a decade earlier. And I could see a crowd. A
heaving, cheering mass; tens of thousands of people had come
to see me jump off New Zealand's highest building. The central
business district was blocked as people flooded into the streets
around the Auckland Sky Tower clamouring to get a view of me
standing on the verge of creating another world record. Massive
spotlights cut through the night sky, lighting me up as I waved to

the television cameras that were broadcasting the jump live to the nation.

I was elated — I felt like some sort of ancient king on a massive pedestal. It's fair to say that the last couple of years had been really hard; dealing with the business split had taken a lot out of me and I seemed to be spending all of my time racing around the world to sort out one mini-disaster after another at our bungy sites. This moment — with the cheering crowd full of excitement and a spectacular leap ahead of me — was confirmation of the intrinsic coolness of bungy. I had taken this strange thing from a daft pastime for a few adrenalin junkies to a large-scale spectacular that brought thousands of people together and made everyone smile. It had gone from the fringes to big business — this jump would launch the new GlobalPlus credit card.

To think that earlier that morning at 5 am, as we went through the final tests on the platform, I had turned to Andy Brinsley — who was part of the crew helping to sort out the mechanics of the jump — and asked: 'Mate, do you think anyone will come to see me do it?'

'Of course, AJ. They'll come to see you. I'm sure of it.'

He didn't sound so sure though. The early morning sky was dark and cloudy and it had rained on and off over the past week as we set up the jump platform and ran our tests. A dash of really bad weather on the night could have seen the whole thing cancelled. The television producers had started preparations to broadcast something else in the event that we couldn't go ahead. Emotionally, I really wanted the jump to be a success, to renew my energies for building up my international operations.

I had been planning this special jump for months. Leaping so close to a major structure meant that I had to develop a cable guideline system to ensure that I wouldn't wrap around the concrete tower on the way down or splat into the side of it. Basically, two strong wires ran along either side of the trajectory down which I would fall. I would be connected to them by free running lines hooked to my waist. The guidelines offered no resistance or protection in case of a broken bungy cord or any other disaster, all they did was keep me away from the tower itself as I fell and rebounded. A rope connected my harness to the guidelines with a couple of little metal rings.

I needed the guidelines so that we could get the jump right for the television broadcast. The weather in Auckland never comes with any guarantees, and it's pretty typical to get gusty, blowy conditions when you least expect them. The slightest bit of wind with a standard bungy would mean that I would have to delay or cancel the jump. Neither option appealed. With a big commercial jump being broadcast live, it was imperative that everything went according to a tight schedule.

Of course, even with no wind, a bungy jumper can track to the left or right a hell of a lot depending on how they make their leap. Too much variation could have seen me splattered down the side of the Sky Tower. Likewise, jumping too far out from the platform could also have serious repercussions with an inward rebound. Using the guide cables meant that I could make the jump in almost any wind.

The plan was to jump directly out from the tower, but I could have jumped the other way, across the line parallel to the structure. Even then we would still have worries with tracking, or a nice gust of wind whipping in off the Waitakere Ranges could wrap me around the building.

For me it was the same old chestnut of accuracy. I wanted to jump and know how far I'd fall, how far I'd bounce on the way back up and how far I'd swing to either side. The sponsors — God bless 'em — wouldn't have sold too many of their swish new credit cards on the back of AJ Hackett mangling and tangling himself down 100 metres of concrete tower in downtown Auckland with thousands of people watching from below and Lord knows how many watching on live television from their sofas at home.

We spent a week setting up the platform and preparing the guidelines. I wanted it to be accurate enough for me to get right down there near the ground, so that the jump was more interesting for the viewing public and for me as a jumper. A ground touch wasn't going to happen, so I had a bundle of balloons set up 15 metres clear of the tarmac and planned to whack into them as hard as I could to raise a cheer from the crowd.

In order for the guideline cables to work, I needed to fall cleanly off the platform — no big hallelujah jump for this one. The plan was for me to drop sweetly, arms straight out to my sides, and tuck straight into a head-first plummet. It would be a very gentle fall from the ledge, so as not to complicate anything with the guidelines.

I bungy jump often. Pretty much every time I visit one of my sites I take a few leaps and, when I jump these days, I'm a pretty cool cucumber. I've done thousands of jumps, so I don't get freaked out like a first-time jumper, and I don't get all cocky like some people who have a dozen jumps under their belts. It's more a matter of process for me. Observing the procedure on the jump deck as the jump-master and the crew potter about, I'll be watching them to make sure they're sharp and on to it. Often I can sense they're a little nervous about having the big boss on board. Then, as the cord is being put on me and I'm getting ready to go, I'll be checking out the actual facilities: the deck, the ropes, the state of the bungy cord. How does the garden next to the pond look from up here? Does the roof of the building need a clean? That sort of thing.

With any business, the best way to understand what your customers are going through and experiencing is to see your operation from their point of view. To take a customer's place and strap yourself in. I suspect that not enough businessmen do this once their enterprise gets to a certain size. Even when I'm in the air, I'm mostly having a wee look about the place — a bungy jump is the ideal time to have a look at the underside of the jump deck and see if that needs a coat of paint.

If you hop in the passenger seat of a rally car and go for a quick burn around a dangerous track, then you would be seriously pumped up but the driver would be completely calm. He's on the job. This is a day at the office for him. It's the same for me with a big jump: all your sensations are switched off and you just concentrate on the few things that are really important. With the jump off the stock exchange building, it was so close to the building that I needed to make sure I whipped myself in and avoided the windows on the rebound. With the Sky Tower jump I simply had to make sure I didn't jump out too far.

Leaping from that Sky Tower for the first time was special. The hairs on the back of my neck were standing up as I took in the sights and the occasion. Even by my been-there-jumped-that standards, this was pretty emotional. It was the atmosphere that got to me.

Things had come a long way since I jumped the stock
exchange building back in 1988, a few hundred yards from where
the Sky Tower now stands. Back then, it was just me and a few
mates, jury-rigging the set-up and tapping bits of wood into the
window frames out of fear that I'd go through one of those glass
window sheets. For the Sky Tower jump, I had a team of experts
with a decade's worth of experience in the industry — all of them
great mates of mine — and a serious budget to build and test the
jump platform and the guidelines.

Standing there on the night, with the adrenalin coursing
through my veins, just as it had all those years ago at the
Greenhithe Bridge, I was really pumped up. I forgot all about
the planned technique for jumping: an easy fall from the edge.
Instead I powered off the platform in an epic swan dive. I leapt
out with my arms splayed and a great smile on face. I was just so
elated — all the people were there below, everything was coming
together and I was getting to do the thing I love to do the most from
the highest structure in my home country. I really felt like it was my
night. So, in the excitement of it all, I instinctively threw myself as
far off the deck as I could. Duh.

I can't really account for it now; I was simply too excited.
I jumped too bloody far.

I leaped out, riding on euphoria, and — whammo — the
guideline cables did their job, catching me and yanking me back
on track, stopping me from going too far out and wrapping around
the tower on the rebound. When the guide cables kicked in, I knew
pretty much straight away what was going on. My torso whipped
around so that I knew what I had to do. I had to get back on target
— get myself lined up so that I was going the right way, with my
head lower than my damn feet which were jerking me about all

over the place. The great concrete tube of the Sky Tower raced past me. The key thing after the jolting start was to make sure I wasn't dropping through rubber. You can get some nasty burns, abrasions and whiplash if you fall into your own bungy cord when doing big jumps like these. In a worst-case scenario you could feasibly get the thing tangled around yourself and then you're in a whole world of trouble. It doesn't happen often — the systems at commercial sites are too well known and the way people jump is too predictable for you to get tangled in your own bungy cable on a small bridge. But off the Sky Tower and with the guide cables jerking me around in different directions, it was a whole new ball game.

I had to get my head facing down so that if there was anything in the way, I could get rid of it on the way down. Pretty soon I was in control of my fall.

Of course from down below it looked like a massive disaster as I was getting jerked about by the guidelines competing with my downward momentum. It all added to the drama for the spectators on the ground as the cables flicked me back and forth, and I twisted around in mid-air to see what was going on. All they could see from the ground was that my body was being flicked about, knocked to and fro, which of course made it all the more spectacular. As soon as I could see that the guidelines were working I knew that I was going to be fine — it would just make for a jolty drop at the top. In truth, the jump wasn't as tight to the tower as it looked — there was actually a bit of room between me and the thing, maybe as much as 15 metres. I thundered downwards, the tower streaking past me and the massive crowd growing larger in my eyes. Then I punched through the balloons to a mighty cheer and gave the thumbs up to all the people below. Perfect.

I'll let you in on a secret. That wasn't the first time I had bungied off the Sky Tower. We had performed three secret early morning test jumps — two on the day before the jump and another early on the morning of the jump itself. I wanted to be sure that the performance was going to be as close to perfect for the television cameras as possible, so when we were through testing with weights, I took the plunge first thing in the morning. High up on the tower, I could hear birdsong as the sun was cutting through the grey light from out east over the Coromandel Peninsula. There was a dull hum from the city as I leaned out and tumbled into a perfect test jump. It was a great rush and an honour to be the first to leap off the Sky Tower.

Having the crowd there for the big event makes things a lot more interesting in terms of putting on a spectacle and giving a real air of excitement, and it's always nice to know that people want to come out and see us do our thing.

But the actual sensation of the jump — the idea of leaping into uncertainty — is a lot more intense the first time that you do it. The first test jump was the morning before the main jump. On the day itself we did another test jump, just to tune it in a bit more and prove to the Sky Tower people and the GlobalPlus crew that everything was sweet.

In the days leading up to it we had terrible weather: wind, rain, even some of those sharp squalls that whip into Auckland off the Pacific. Some strong winds were knocking the weight bags about in the test drops, but I would have jumped it in any conditions. If there was a major issue with safety we could always pull the pin, but I was confident that we'd done the business properly in the build-up. Unfortunately (but understandably), the GlobalPlus sponsors and the Sky Tower people themselves had the power to pull the pin, so I was left praying for good conditions to stop them from freaking out. I found myself spending a lot of time reassuring the Sky Tower management in particular that I had no intention of dying beneath their tower.

The biggest part of the testing was to make sure the guide runners weren't going to jam or break. Theoretically, if one side broke then you'd end up wrapped around the other cable, while still falling. Not a good look.

Weight tests do two things: firstly, there's sorting out the rigging system — how we get the bungy cords back up and all that sort of stuff — and, obviously, the lengths involved in terms of the bungy cord. All that raising and lowering — the physical side of things. We did one weight drop on the first morning of testing and did two the second morning with the new weight. After each test drop, we tuned everything and checked the cords to see if they had stretched at all. We tuned it all and lowered the ropes down just to get everything a little bit more accurate.

The car park beneath the casino proved an ideal workshop for making and measuring the bungy cord. Three weight tests is enough, unless you're encountering some sort of problem. It gets to a point at which you're not going to achieve any more by throwing weights off, and at some stage you've got to make the call. Everyone was pretty happy, so I stepped up and told the boys that it was time for a jump. A test jump would also confirm the timing we needed to work in with the television crews, so I jumped it to see if there was anything else to be worked on. The main thing I was watching for was resistance from the guidelines, but there was none. That first test jump also gave us a chance to get the recovery boys down the bottom organised so they knew what was going on and what they had to do, again to appease the timing of the television gods.

The very last test jump, performed on the morning of the main jump itself, was the final opportunity to pull out. At that point any of the parties involved — GlobalPlus, Sky City or me — could have pulled the pin. Thankfully, everyone held their nerve.

The Sky Tower jump happened pretty soon after the split between me and Henry van Asch, so I sorted out a crew of my own to help organise the jump, independently of Henry and his Queenstown operation. I wanted a good team of people I could trust, so I had Adam Lichtenstein, Mike Champoux and Geoffrey Wilson, along with Hippy and Andy Brinsley, our old managers who by this stage were running the Pipeline Bungy. There was still some bad blood between Henry and the Pipeline boys, but it was really nice that Henry came up for the weight tests. Henry knew the Sky Tower would be a great site to jump; he'd expressed interest in doing a bungy from it at the time the tower opened in 1997, but the Sky City people were a little wary at that stage.

I had good people on my side throughout this project. It was Andy Haden, the former All Black great, who now seems to have a hand in pretty much every major celebrity portfolio in New Zealand, who first put me onto GlobalPlus, negotiating a deal for me to feature in some ads for their new credit card. Andy has done a lot of my deals over the years, and seems to have an uncanny fix on the celebrity currency in New Zealand. It was while we were shooting the ads that Rick Stevens, the account manager for Colenso and an old school buddy, mentioned that they were looking for a way to launch the new card and he wondered if I would consider jumping off the Sky Tower.

'Consider it? I'd love it!'

From there we had just two months to fast track the process of planning and organising the jump — a huge task. In the days leading up to the jump we were all staying in the Sky City hotel at the base of the tower. We had fabulous suites and — unwisely on the part of the Sky City operators — we all had open bar tabs. Suffice to say when we finished our testing and preparations early each morning the old bungy team spent a fair bit of energy exploring precisely what the Sky City management team had meant when they used the term 'open bar tab'. Things had certainly come a long way since I had evaded security guards and slept rough overnight in order to jump off the Eiffel Tower.

We'd wrap up on the site sometime after 6 am and head for the bar or one of the fella's rooms. It's the quietest time of day, so naturally there was a fairly steady flow of people tiptoeing out of hotel rooms they weren't meant to be in. One bloke backed out of a room gingerly and turned around to see half-a-dozen of us laden with karabiners and bungy cords. 'Nice night for it,' said Hippy.

Naturally, by the end of our week in the hotel we managed to pin down the exact meaning of the term 'open bar tab'.

Sky City were incredibly nervous about the jump. In the days leading up to the event their representatives would come along and peer out at us setting everything up. As the actual launch date neared, they became even more fretful. This is understandable, as they had a pretty unusual gig taking place on their nice shiny tower. We expended a lot of energy soothing their concerns and placating some of the people high up in the management system there.

The success of the jump was great for the Sky Tower people. For them it was all about timing — the tower had been open for over a year and the spectacle gave them a nice boost of publicity and got them back on the front pages of all the papers. We were amazed at how quickly the attitudes of some of their staff changed. They went in a flash from regarding us with great caution — almost suspicion — to hugging us in relief and grabbing every photo opportunity along the way. Today there's an adventure-tourism operator up there running a business with an aided jump that gives customers a nice, safe drop to the ground below; kind of similar to a bungy but without quite the freefall buzz and with no rebound. It was the success of the GlobalPlus launch that opened up the possibility of installing the Skyjump on the tower. Today I work closely with the Skyjump operators, Steve Weidmann and Nick Andreef, to distribute their product globally.

Just how worried the Sky Tower people were about something going wrong came to light a few hours before I was to make the jump. Hippy was in the management office tying up a couple of loose ends when he came across three different press releases that had been prepared by the PR people handling the media stuff connected with the jump. Each of the three press releases was ready to be sent out. The first one said: 'AJ Hackett has set a new bungy jump record, leaping off the Auckland Sky Tower.' The second one said: 'AJ Hackett has been injured breaking the world record for bungy jumping.' And the last one said: 'Sadly AJ is dead.'

CHAPTER 12

The ties
that bind

A couple of weeks before I bungy jumped off the Eiffel Tower I
met the woman who was to become my wife. Some mutual friends
introduced me to a Frenchwoman called Caroline in a restaurant
one day in Paris and we hit it off straight away, although right
from the outset she felt pretty sure that I was completely mad
for bouncing around attached to pieces of rubber. At the time,
she was working as a model and was on the road a lot, living in
Germany and London, but she'd returned to Paris to visit family
and friends.

Madcap though my Eiffel Tower scheme appeared, she
was intrigued and within a couple of hours of meeting her, I
was writing Caroline into the plan for the top secret overnight
operation that came prior to the jump itself. This was how Caroline
and a good friend found themselves carrying the bungies up the
tower in backpacks and later using their models' looks to effect

with some fluttering of eyelashes to distract the security guards.

That night after she left me with the overnight crew sleeping amid the rafters up on the Eiffel Tower, Caroline walked away with friends and had a good laugh about the daft Kiwi she had just met. She returned the next morning to see me jump. I'm sure the jump made quite an impression on her, but it made rather more of an impression on the gendarmes, who dragged me off to a paddy wagon as soon as I got down. As I've said, to stay out of trouble with the law, I had already arranged to leave France immediately after the bungy and return to New Zealand, where I had plans to take up some building work and have a go at opening a ski shop down in Ohakune. So that was it for Caroline and I, our Parisian romance was over almost as soon as it had begun. But eight months later, I returned to France for another ski season and we ran into each other again. From then on Caroline and I were together for sixteen years.

The first few years we were together were incredibly hectic as the business was developing at a fast pace. We got married at a registry office in Auckland on 8 September 1988. Because none of her family could be there for the wedding, I decided not to have any of mine there, so we had a fast, fun wedding with two good friends as witnesses, and plenty of champagne, but today we don't have a single photo of the wedding. We had a camera and we had the film but we also had more champagne than perhaps we ought to have consumed and in the excitement we didn't take a single photo.

We went down to Ohakune for a while where Chris Allum and I were running our New Sensations ski shop. It was down there that Caroline did her first bungy jump, at the bridge near Ohakune where we were to eventually open for the first commercial jumps. She knew bungy was a big deal for me, and that I hoped to do something grand with it somehow, but she was certainly nervous the first time she jumped. She was shaking all over before the jump but afterwards she was wired, and giggled for a long time.

I could see that Caroline wasn't happy staying in Ohakune — it's a long way from the catwalks of Europe — and I was already thinking about distant pastures. My time in France had stayed in my mind and even then I felt that at some point Caroline and I would head for her homeland — but first there was a bungy empire to launch.

Caroline and I spent most of our first winter together shuttling between Ohakune and Auckland. When we opened down in Queenstown in November 1988, Caroline was perched in this little white caravan, roughly the size of a shoebox, but not quite as warm on a cold Central Otago winter's day. She handled sales and bookings for the jumps off the Kawarau Bridge, while Henry van Asch and I took care of business on the bridge itself.

Today, Caroline remembers the caravan with what I like to think of as fondness. 'It was a run-down piece of rubbish. A jalopy that someone had loaned us. The whole thing had this wild side to it; this sort of gypsy feeling. Working out of the caravan and then moving on. It was a bit rough. It wasn't about making things look pretty.'

The caravan could be the scene of some pretty intense cabin fever. One of the worst arguments I have ever heard came about when Caroline had a spring clean of the caravan and ripped some old posters off the walls and threw them out. Turns out that Henry had been particularly fond of one of these posters — he's always been a car nut, and this was a picture of his favourite car. Pretty soon the two of them were nose-to-nose, prodding fingers in each other's chests and delving at length into each other's moral and personal failings. For five intense minutes, our little caravan shook to the rhythm of their anger. Having had some pretty fulsome rows over the last couple of decades with both Henry and Caroline, I can assure you that this was not a battlefield to step into lightly.

When the dust had settled I bought them both a drink to cool things down, but they didn't speak to each other for three days.

In those early days at Queenstown, Henry may have felt that things were piled against him as it was always two against one. Caroline and I were a couple and although the staff were old mates of both Henry and me, it's fair to say that I had more of my family involved in the business, as my sister Elaine was also on the team.

We didn't stay very long in Queenstown. As much as we loved the beautiful town tucked in between the Southern Alps and the lake, we often felt trapped there. I still love to visit as often as I can, but it just felt too small to put down roots. So once the business was ticking over in Ohakune, we sold the house we had in Auckland and headed off to France where we settled in Paris and took an apartment. I loved the lifestyle and the sense of living in a new culture.

A pattern started to develop almost as soon as we got back to

France: something would go a bit pear-shaped in Queenstown and I'd have to race back there, often at very short notice. Henry was good at dealing with stuff on the ground but for some of the bigger things, I just had to be back there. If there were consent hearings to be sorted out with the local council or the Department of Conservation or if there was publicity stuff to be done, the punters expected to see AJ Hackett walking around the place. So I would fly out to New Zealand, leaving Caroline behind, and if it wasn't New Zealand, it was Australia, where the franchise holders were about to set up in Cairns.

Married to a Frenchwoman and with a growing love of the country, I really felt I needed to set up a bungy site in my adopted country to put down some roots. After a year in Paris, I had found the abandoned, run-down railway viaduct in Normandy where I knew I could build a beautiful bungy site. We shifted out to Normandy together where we found a nice house I could tinker around in. They were hectic days, and somewhere between racing back to Queenstown for DOC hearings and climbing about building my new bungy site in Normandy, Caroline and I found out that we were going to have a baby.

The Normandy site was shaping up nicely but things were still hectic for us when Caroline was nearly due with our first child. We went back to Paris and rented a flat near the hospital, allowing ourselves a couple of weeks to buy some clothes for the baby and get everything set up. Or so we thought. When we dropped in to see the doctor upon our arrival in Paris, he said: 'You're not going anywhere. You're about to have your baby.' Caroline went straight from his office to a room in the hospital and our son Dean was born the very next day.

She ended up in hospital for about ten days, and rather than stay in this rented flat by myself, I set up a bunk in the maternity room alongside Caroline and Dean. With things heating up in Australia and the site in Normandy developing nicely, I couldn't just ignore my business so I brought the business with me, setting up a corner of the maternity room with my papers and even a fax machine. The nurses would be running around taking messages — 'Mr Hackett, it's Australia on the phone for you' — and some of the first sounds my son ever heard were those of his father trying to hold the liquidators in Cairns at bay over the telephone while his mother tut-tutted. Start as you mean to go on, they say.

It's not easy being a part of my life. I constantly make myself busy and am very driven about running my businesses. Every year I would tell Caroline the same thing: 'Darling it's going to be tough this year; I'll be incredibly busy, but when we're done with all this it'll be straight forward.' I never meant to repeat the message; each year I really thought I would have all the bungy sites sorted out and be in a position to relax.

Normandy was beautiful, but I had always wanted to live in the mountains, so we spent a few years looking out for a place in the French Alps. I had a dream of renovating and settling in an old French farmhouse on a hillside. With Dean a new arrival, Caroline and I spent a couple of years keeping an eye out for the right house. On one trip to the Alps, a real estate agent said he had a couple of places we might like.

'They are both beautiful old farmhouses. One of them is very easy to get to and the other one . . . well it's a bit of a 4 x 4 thing.'

My ears pricked up at that, and as soon as I saw the house

I had visions of settling in it. But it was certainly a 4 x 4 thing, accessible only by a winding track, heavily snowed in during the winter and rutted with holes all year round.

'It's a lovely spot,' Caroline said. 'But we can't live here, AJ.'

I was in stubborn mode. I was adamant that this would be our dream home. It was completely private, the views were incredible and the old farmhouse was pretty much untouched, so for a chippy it was ideal. The house promised the dream life of a chalet in the mountains and an international getaway via Geneva, which was only an hour away.

It also promised obscurity. I'm a private kind of guy and as much as I'm always really flattered to have someone recognise me and want to talk about my work or my business, it can get pretty tiring to always be AJ Hackett — Mr Bungy. Living on an isolated hillside in the French Alps I could just be AJ, husband and father.

'And I'll do something about the driveway, honey. Promise.'

I brought some friends down from Normandy to help work on the farmhouse, which was pretty much a shell when we took it over. By November 1993, we had knocked the house into shape and fitted it out with the basics so that the family could move in. Cold doesn't begin to describe it. The underfloor heating took a long time to warm the place and we decided we wanted gas, not oil. But no one wanted to deliver gas up to the house. There was only one room that was warm enough to live in, so the three of us slept in the same bed, shivering. But in the first few years we didn't spend so much time there in the winter — we always seemed to be out in New Zealand or Australia.

And I kept promising to fix the driveway.

Ah, the driveway.

Caroline was a trooper. She put up with what I guess you
could call 'guy stuff'. Take the driveway, for instance. Mates tell
me I could sell tickets at the bottom of our driveway and call it an
extreme 4 x 4 off-road adventure track — I guess they're right too.
When we bought this farmhouse in the French Alps, I knew that I
would need a great beast of an off-roader to have any chance of
getting up the steep, grinding turns and fighting through the mud
and snow. The first 4 x 4 I ran up there was a bright green Lada
— we spent many a happy afternoon cursing at that thing. Later
we graduated to cursing at a Land Rover. With chains on the Land
Rover we generally made it up the hill okay, but on a really bad
day — after a thick dump of snow — we'd have to use the winch
on the front of the thing to haul the vehicle up the driveway. The
longest it's ever taken me to get up the 500 metre driveway is two
hours — it's not your normal commute home. Even at the best of
times, the driveway was steep, slippery and pocked with deep
potholes.

If I wasn't around, then poor Caroline had to drive the Land
Rover as far up the incline as it would go, then get out at one or
two of the trickier points and walk to tie the cable around a strong
tree. Then back down to the Land Rover where she would use the
motorised winch, gun the engine a bit and lurch up the hill. On
really snowy days she remembers having to do this two or three
times to get up to the house. 'Thank God we had no neighbours
because sometimes I'd be hysterically screaming at the bloody
vehicle and the bloody driveway. I'd be carrying the baby in the
backpack with a backpack full of groceries on the front and the
baby's shoe would fall off and I'd have to walk back down to get it.
Looking back, it was crazy but at the time I didn't question it — this

173

was my house, I had to get my babies into the house and care for them and make the house a home.'

I tried to be at home with the family during the winter months as much as I could, because of the tough haul getting up the driveway (and because the skiing is great). Of course, every time I went away on a business trip, there would be a thick dump of snow, trapping Caroline at home. It probably didn't help her mood to consider that while she was weighed down with snow and freezing cold, my business trips were to sunny Acapulco and Bali. By the time our second son, Jayde, was born the house was properly kitted out, but access was still tough. Some days the Land Rover would simply be left at the end of the driveway, leaving a 20 minute trek through deep snow to get up to the house.

Now blokes love this sort of stuff: messing around with winches and engines and racing about in snowdrifts; it's a boy's own adventure. But it's maybe not so much fun for a young mother running the house alone while her husband is away on a business trip, with her two young boys at her side while her arms are laden with shopping. Suffice to say, we didn't make the decision to pop out to the corner store to buy a bottle of milk lightly.

I kept telling Caroline that next year everything would be easier. Then, what do you know, another kid was on the way. She said to me: 'You can't have this home in the mountains with everything radical and getting up the driveway a big adventure AND have it as a family home with three little kids in it.'

In the worst winter we had up in the hills, even winching the Land Rover — which constantly broke down anyway — was no good. We ran out of gas in the middle of one of the coldest winters on record, with thick snow piling up all round and we couldn't get more gas bottles up the hill to the house. For two months I couldn't even drive my Unimog truck up the hill to the house — so we slogged uphill through the snow. Thankfully, this neighbour from down the hill came and helped us out, using his old farm horse to haul up the gas bottles. The Land Rover was a sorry sight tucked in on the side of the road as the stocky workhorse did its job.

This driveway tells you something about me and how I deal with the world. My business life is very full on and different from the norm, and I operate very differently from other people. Now in order to navigate this driveway you have to fully focus on what you're doing. It completely clears everything out of my head. The driveway is a pretty effective barrier too. None of those encyclopedia salesmen are going to find their way up here to test their wits against the former master of their trade. For a lot of people it's completely inaccessible — for me it's totally accessible.

I tried my best to work to a three-week rule: if I was away for more than three weeks I would take the whole family with me. I only broke the rule a few times.

After our third child — our beautiful girl Margaux — was born on 2 June 1999, we travelled as a family for six months while I worked in Mexico, Bali and Australia, dropping into New Zealand to see my mum as well. It was wonderful to have the kids and Caroline on the road with me for such a long time, but there was a cost that came with my constant travelling to deal with the business. Caroline was shouldering more than her share of raising the kids and she was providing a stable core for me. We were a team and doing a lot of exciting stuff. With me travelling so much it was always wonderful to catch up again but increasingly it would take us longer and longer to adjust to each other after I'd been on the road for a few weeks. I always juggled to keep an equilibrium between family, business and my own personal life, the part of me that wanted to go skiing alone, or to the pub with a mate. It became clear that the business was winning.

In 2003, we separated. This was the most traumatic thing I've confronted in my life. It totally freaked me out, as I had always believed Caroline and I would be bound for a lifelong commitment. Separation is painful; it was tough enough making sense of what was going on myself. I found it incredibly hard, crying with my son and trying to reassure the kids that we loved them more than ever and that Daddy and Mummy still loved each other but simply couldn't live together happily. Fortunately, we've remained the best of friends and Caroline lives nearby, so the kids get all the time they need with both of us. We have different parenting styles — guess which of us is the one who forgets that the kids need dinner and actually you can't just take them out of school for the day just because you're flying out tomorrow.

Some ties continue to bind. Until recently Caroline was still doing some of my financial bookkeeping and taking care of the administration stuff I got bogged down on.

Here's a little tip for anyone faced with the painful process of a divorce: set the terms early. And I don't mean who gets what property and what access to the dog and kids — I mean the terms by which you commit to divorcing as painlessly as possible. It sounds cold, but when Caroline and I first realised that we might be heading towards a separation, we drew up an agreement about how we would handle things if worst came to worst. Divorce wasn't actually upon us at that stage, but it seemed a distinct possibility. We sat down one evening and talked about the things

ABOVE: *Caroline relaxing,
Queenstown style.*

RIGHT: *Margaux about to
become the youngest girl
to bungy jump in Bali at
the age of four.*

ABOVE: *Jumping over rainforest, Cairns.*

BELOW: *Sunset surfboard jumping, Bali.*

Bless all those who jump

LEFT: The Red Hot Chilli Peppers' Anthony Kiedis about to make a tropical bungy jump in Cairns.

BELOW: Cairns tower, Queensland, Australia. The world's first purpose built bungy tower.

RIGHT: *Almost there! Mast climbers near the top of Macau Tower.*

BELOW: *The family chilling Gili Trawangan style, Indonesia, 2006.*

that mattered most to us: our kids and their future. Over a bottle of wine, we wrote down some commitments that we would stick to if things ever got really rough. It was based on the love of our children, and the love and respect we had for each other. By writing these terms down when we were still communicating properly (and not at each other throats), it meant that when dark days came upon us, we had a common foundation to which we could return. It also meant that we could clear our heads and have another go at salvaging our relationship.

Later, when separation was inevitable, we both stayed true to our pact. There's no easy way to divorce, and I'm lucky that Caroline and I managed to cling to some of the good things from our relationship through those tough times.

I'll let Caroline have the last word. 'There was no option for us to handle the separation in any way other than what was best for the kids,' she says. 'We're still a massive part of each other's lives and I can't imagine life without our friendship. We are the best of friends and I know if either of us ever needs anything then the other will always be there to help.'

CHAPTER 13

Safety
first

No one has ever died on an AJ Hackett Bungy site. I am immensely proud of that fact. More than two million people have jumped from our bungy platforms around the world but we have never had a death. We've had a couple of close calls, and we've had a few eager punters end up soaked and battered from water touches that went in a bit too hard, but no deaths. Touch wood. From the very first time I went jumping with Chris Sigglekow, launching off the Greenhithe Bridge, I was more interested in the interesting psychological challenge of controlling the physical elements than just pure thrill seeking. I was an experienced rock climber and so the safety element was paramount for me. Whereas others, say the Oxford University Dangerous Sports Club, would say to themselves, 'I wonder what's going to happen if I jump off this bridge?'; for me the question was always, 'How do I jump off this bridge safely?'

Yet, the industry in which we operate is inherently dangerous; the activity we promote and sell invites risk. Our challenge and ultimately our greatest triumph has been to control that danger; to master the risk. Me, Henry and everyone who has ever worked alongside us can take great pride from the safety record of AJ Hackett Bungy. It's a record that is the envy of other adventure tourism operators in New Zealand and around the world.

When bungy first took off, there was a period of a few years when a lot of people died while jumping on sites run by cowboy operators. The first bungy deaths I heard of in France came in the year after I had left, following that seminal winter at the Pont de la Caille. I felt awful — this wonderful thing that I had brought into France and introduced to a select group of friends had spread uncontrolled and ultimately claimed someone's life. A part of me felt I had some degree of responsibility; I even wondered if I should stop promoting and pushing bungy. But the more I learnt about the fly-by-night operators, the more I was outraged by the way they ran their businesses and the more I felt determined to push on and force my standards onto the burgeoning sport.

The French all wanted to do the best, the biggest, the fastest, the most radical — and of course to get the most sponsorship money from outdoor sports companies. In their enthusiasm to try new, extreme experiences, a lot of people simply weren't thinking things through properly. They started having accidents pretty much as soon as they started bungying. One woman did a huge bungy from a hot-air balloon with about a 600–700 metre stretch. That's a massive jump. And of course the balloon wasn't tethered. She ended up dangling there as the balloon slowly moved away until she was dragged underneath some high-tension power cables. The balloon was over the wires and continued to edge along and it started to drag her up into these cables. They cut the power just in time, and they got her down after about 45 minutes, but she was incredibly lucky to survive.

Others were less fortunate. There was a period in France in which there were three deaths within about two months. One of them was a woman who died while doing a reverse bungy at a crane set up where they were hooked to the ground using a sort of slingshot mechanism, with the cord stretching taut above them. When the connection holding them down was released, the passenger would launch into the air at a great rate of knots. A large male had gone on the bungy slingshot before the woman, and of course he weighed a lot more. So she stepped up for her turn — weighing maybe 20 kilograms less than the guy — and they kept the same bloody cord geared up for the same tension. She simply hurtled into the boom of the crane, received massive head injuries and died that day.

It was unsurprising when the French government stepped in and banned bungy, but disappointing all the same. Boom, it was illegal in France — where I happened to be living at the time — for about three or four years. Eventually they made it legal again but with some very tight restrictions.

Perhaps the most famous bungy death of all time was the unfortunate case of Michael Lush, who was picked out of a live audience at a BBC television programme called the *Late, Late Breakfast Show* and challenged to do a bungy jump in order to win some sort of prize. In a rehearsal for the jump, a clip apparently came loose, and this 25-year-old guy hit the deck hard and died on the spot. This was November 1986, before any of my big publicity jumps, and a member of the Oxford University Dangerous Sports Club had been running the jump along with a stunt coordinator from the BBC. Neither of them knew enough to run a jump properly and the whole thing had been cobbled together in a very rough fashion.

In those early days, you could buy a mail order bungy kit from Europe. You sent off your cheque and a box would come out in the post with a bungy cord, some ties and karabiners and a one page sheet of instructions. One page! My jaw still drops just to think of it. We spend years training our jump-masters and here was a business making a profit by kidding people into thinking they knew what they were doing on the basis of one page of instructions. The idiots who bought this set would rig up their bungy following their one page of instructions but would not have the common sense to realise that the cord shouldn't be rubbing against a concrete wall or that the cord should be stored in a dry space. The concept of a mail order bungy set goes against everything I've set out to do with bungy. You have to have the highest standards possible, and that's not achieved by posting out a rubber cord and a sheet of paper to any moron with a chequebook.

At least the home bungy kit was mostly used by people just doing a few jumps for themselves so the chances were that they would only hurt themselves. But the fly-by-night operators in the US were another kettle of fish. Often some guy who owned a crane or had a mate with one that they could hire cheaply at the end of a working week would set up a bungy operation for Saturdays and Sundays. During the week the guy would be working nine to five down at the factory or selling insurance, or whatever, but come the weekend, this same guy was at the forefront of the adventure tourism industry. An instant bungy pioneer. And he would be completely clueless.

A lot of these weekend operators never had the customer numbers to justify turning over their equipment. We would generally throw away bungies after about 300–400 jumps, even though they would be good for several thousand more. A commercial set-up that only runs for a few days a month simply couldn't justify buying new cords and karabiners so often. Likewise, they didn't have the turnover to justify training staff.

We used to make all our own bungies ourselves but in the States it was standard for the cords to be bought fully made up. In the US most jump-masters worked from a colour-coded book. They followed the numbers but had no instinct for it. Really good jump-masters will be able to make their own cords and judge someone's weight and all that without following a guidebook.

Eventually the bungy market cleaned itself up. There simply weren't enough punters to go around so the first lot of cowboys to enter the industry buggered off back to selling used cars or whatever it was they did for a day job. Overnight the accidents stopped happening and from the mid-1990s onwards the industry has been a lot safer.

Of course, New Zealand's bungy industry was not immune to shoddy operators. People came out to the Kawarau Bridge and saw what we were doing and thought it looked like an easy way to make money. So they went away and many of them found out the hard way — by hurting people — that bungy requires a lot of specialist knowledge.

The only bungy fatality to happen in New Zealand to date occurred at Rainbow's End amusement park in Auckland. The

operator there was a company called Heavy Rubber and they
had nothing to do with AJ Hackett Bungy. They ran a small, high-
turnover tower, with jumps costing about $25 a go. After a day of
operating in February 1990, the jump-master and some friends
were hanging around on the site. They were smoking cannabis.
Not a good mix.

The jump-master was a 22 year old called Jason Collett. He
was in charge on the scene and never should have let anyone
near the tower or the ropes given the state that they were all in.
His mate Thomas Hemi and another friend up the tower tossed a
coin to decide which of them would be the first to take a bungy
jump. Hemi, who had also been smoking cannabis, won the coin
toss. When he jumped, he would not even have been aware that
the cord attached to his ankles was not properly connected to
the tower; it was merely looped over a storage hook. Hemi was
nineteen, and he hit the deck with no resistance to break his
fall. He died 20 minutes later; some members of his family were
there with him as he passed away. Collett was later convicted
of manslaughter and the judge said he had been 'unacceptably
lackadaisical' on the tower. What happened there was a stain
on our industry and added to my already powerful desire to make
bungy safe for all.

Another dodgy operator had already had a very close call
when they were working a crane jump at Mt Smart Stadium, also
in Auckland. There, in October 1989, a trainee staff member came
out of a harness and took a heavy, though not fatal, fall, so their
standards were clearly lacking from the outset.

In the wrong hands, bungy is quite simply lethal. There have
been no other bungy deaths in New Zealand since this one
unfortunate — and completely avoidable — case. Given that our

little country is the bungy capital of the world, the fact that there has been just the one fatality (and that on a site run by someone no longer in the business) comes as something of a relief.

Whether in Bali or Queenstown, Normandy or Cairns, Henry and I have always had the highest standards when it comes to looking after our customers. We have been fortunate to have had staff right from day one who were also very firm on what needed to be done.

When we appointed Glenn Russell — Hippy — as our international operations manager, his number one priority was to maintain the highest standard across the board at all of our sites. We took the New Zealand Standards system (NZ5848, to those in the business) that we had developed and shipped it to the world, hoping it would be used across the industry globally.

Hippy was also busy keeping an eye on rivals in the New Zealand market. When he visited some short-term operators running what proved to be a temporary site from a bridge near Taupo, he was happy to note that the jump-master and all the guys on the jump platform were wearing safety harnesses. 'Good stuff,' thought Hippy. 'That's the AJ Hackett influence coming through.'

As Hippy wandered out onto the jump platform to say hello and have a closer inspection of their set-up, he realised that the shiny new safety harnesses — though replete with karabiners — were not actually hooked up to anything.

'Er . . . fellas, why are you guys wearing those harnesses?'

'Well, we saw you guys using them in Queenstown, mate. And

we thought they looked pretty good!'

'Did you know that we have our harnesses hooked to the platform?'

'Huh?'

Jump-masters at a site in Japan did a similar thing. The staff up on a jump platform at an amusement park near Nagoya wore harnesses but, like Hippy's mates near Taupo, the harnesses were not actually connected to anything. One of our guys actually saw this site while passing through Japan in 1995. Sure enough, two weeks after our guy had passed through, a novice jumper went over the edge, panicked, and grabbed the jump-master, pulling him over the side. As he fell, the jump-master managed to hook an arm on to the edge of the platform and his body swung under it. But he lost his grip and fell to his death, swinging inward to the tower's base. Perversely, if he had not caught his hand on the platform, he may have survived by landing on the back-up airbag below, as it was the motion of swinging beneath the platform that took him away from the airbag. Of course the other thing that certainly would have kept this guy alive was if one of the karabiners on his harness had been connected to something secure on the platform.

Some operators never learn. Many people remember the Swiss canyoning disaster that claimed the lives of 21 people in 1999. Probably fewer people are aware that the company responsible for the loss of life in that tragedy, Adventure World, sent a young bungy jumper to his death less than a year later. The business operated a gondola jump in Interlaken and in May 2000 an American traveller, Matthew Coleman, went for a jump. Their system was simple: they offered two jumps, one from 100 metres and one from 180 metres. The gondola would simply stop at the appropriate height and the jumper would have one of two cords attached, depending on the height they were jumping from. Simple enough, right? What could possibly go wrong? Well, for one thing the gondola could be parked at 100 metres while the bloke is hooked up to the cord for the 180-metre jump. Coleman died instantly as four of his mates looked on from the gondola. Thankfully these guys are no longer operating.

Some people continue to find ways to operate even after being responsible for causing the death of innocent paying customers. One operator in France hides behind various associates and continues to offer his services even after two clients died in separate incidents at different sites.

When Andy Brinsley and Hippy opened the Pipeline, they felt the added weight of responsibility that goes with owning a site. 'One of my worst nightmares,' says Hippy, 'was that someone would come out of the harness and we'd kill them. Imagine trying to explain to someone how you'd killed their son. We were well-drilled on the safety stuff at Kawarau, but you feel it more when the buck stops with you.'

I had felt it since day one, but today, of any adventure tourism experience, bungy is probably the safest that there is. Look at rafting, hang-gliding and parachuting. There's a much higher turnover with bungy — more people are going through with only four or five minutes per jump. Three minutes if you really crank it up on a busy day. The fact that there haven't been a lot more fatalities is pretty impressive.

Of course, even at AJ Hackett Bungy we have had some close

calls. The first time someone got hurt jumping with one of my
rigs was back in the early days when Chris Sigglekow and I
took a bunch of mates for a bungy session and a picnic at one of
those big central North Island rail viaducts, way before we went
professional. By this stage the core group was growing, mates like
Chris Allum were regulars. Everywhere we went, more friends
would come along for a look. On the day of our champagne
picnic, there was great food and a great atmosphere. Everyone
did a jump with the parachute harness and when they were
comfortable with that, we let them have a go with the cord hooked
at their ankles, diving out, in what has become the classic bungy
jump swallow-dive. I was getting pretty cocky about all this and
had discovered a knack for figuring out an impromptu calculation
combining how much someone weighed with how far out they
would jump, so that I could get people swooping in pretty close to
the water, just a foot or so off it.

The key is that they have to do a big dive out, so the cord will
swing, meaning there'll be sideways movement, instead of a
plummeting drop straight down. The wines were flowing and the
picnic was lovely when this old mate of mine, Kingsley Turner, got
up there. He had jumped really well with the parachute harness
and I expected a massive dive out from the bridge with the foot tie.
Instead dear old Kingsley sort of froze as he leaned forward into
his dive. He just kept leaning and leaning; completely frozen. But
he didn't dive until the last moment, at which point he was almost
pointing downwards. I was standing side-on, muttering 'Oh no,
oh no, oh no' as Kingsley froze. I knew immediately what would
happen.

Kingsley pretty much propelled himself downwards like a
missile. He hit the water hard. Then he hit the rocky bottom of

the river hard. When the bungy yanked him back up out of the water, he had cut his head open and there was blood gushing everywhere. We raced him to a nearby hospital with a little story that I had already made up about how he had taken a wee fall while rock climbing. Real imaginative cover-up that one. And at least it had a ring of truth to it . . . well, he fell and there were rocks.

Thankfully, Kingsley was all right, but his splash-down pretty much put a damper on things. And with the memory of my close call at the Pont de la Caille also nagging me, we cooled off on doing long jump sessions with friends and champagne for quite some time afterwards.

Scrapes and bruises with your mates are one thing, but injuries at a commercial operation are another matter altogether. Our first really serious, 'oh-my-god-what-have-we-done' accident operating as a bona fide business came in our first winter based in Queenstown, in July 1989. We were doing a group bungy for the Winter Festival. Now, I've always felt that group jumps are by nature riskier; when you have more people involved you have more opportunity for things to go wrong. Simple as that. But this was our first Winter Festival and being the new kids in town we felt we had to do something really spectacular. There was a lot of hype about the bungy operation, people were starting to see that we could offer a bright new future for tourism in and around Queenstown. And we had a real buzz about us; we knew we were on to something really special. We wanted to do something for the festival befitting of our sudden superstar status in the town. A group jump seemed like a great idea.

Which is all well and good, but somehow there was a stuff-up.

Our team was to jump from a cage elevated by a crane, right at the peak of the festival. It wasn't a huge jump, just over 30 metres, but with ten people planning to leap simultaneously from three platforms we were confident it would look pretty impressive.

One of the guys working for us in the very first winter in Queenstown was a pretty gung-ho guy called Moki. On the day of the event, we were doing some final tests out at a building site, when Moki decided to make a last-minute alteration to his gear, to allow himself some room to do a couple of little somersaults on the way down. Moki undid his own rig and refitted it, without anyone else checking it. Naughty boy. As best as we can figure, Moki must have missed a loop with the karabiner when he hooked himself back up.

Hippy jumped with Moki when he hurt himself. The pair leapt alongside one another but at the point where their cords were fully extended (maximum loading) the webbing connecting Moki to the bungy unravelled. Gravity took over and Moki dropped eight metres to the ground. There was a massive crack up the top as Moki's cord whacked into the underside of the cage, smashing a few bits of timber. 'I thought something had busted up there,' says Hippy. 'So when I saw Moki fall, I thought that I was going down next because I figured something had busted up top.'

Moki hit the deck hard. It was not a pretty sight. He was in hospital for several weeks afterwards and basically looked like a human bruise, but he came through with no permanent damage, and Moki remains one of life's special characters. That was a test jump so we all had a lengthy chat to decide if we should go ahead with the jump at the festival. We decided that since we knew what had happened — and it wasn't a gear malfunction, it

was something that Moki had done to his own rig — we should go
ahead with it. Five of the team jumped for the actual event and it
was a great success.

Maintaining excellent communication throughout your business
is the best way to prevent stuff-ups. In a two month period around
the time of the split between Henry and myself, we had three
major accidents at AJ Hackett Bungy sites involving customers.
This was at an awkward time for the business as Henry and I were
drifting further and further apart.

In September 1996, a customer at our site in Bali (a Hong
Kong-based Irish nurse) fell 3.5 metres into the water when there
was an equipment failure. The Bali crew had received a batch
of bungies from New Zealand with new 'bobbins' — that's the
key link between the ties around the jumper's lower leg and the
actual bungy cord — which were designed to replace our older
heavier metal and Teflon ones. The new bobbins were sent from
Queenstown where they were being used as standard. The
problem was that the bobbins sent to Bali did not arrive with a
crucial connecting webbing, so the Bali crew assumed they were
meant to thread the standard 25 millimetre tubular webbing cord
through the bobbin. They were wrong. In New Zealand a single 12
millimetre loop was being used, which allowed the bobbin to still
act as a hinge. Doubling up 25 millimetre webbing for additional
security simply blocked the critically important hinging effect.
The result was the bungy cord lasted only 120 jumps and then
completely snapped.

Once the cord had snapped, this heavy, thoroughly stretched

bungy basically became a deadly whip. Having broken at the jumper's end the thick rubber lashed at lightning speed back up to the jump platform. We were bloody lucky because the cord whipped back up and slammed into the underside of the platform, splitting three of the wooden boards. If the staff up there had been peering over the side then there would have been a decapitation on the cards. The site has a four metre deep pool under the jump zone. The pool is designed for water touches and as back-up safety so the client had a swim instead of the usual rebound.

Some years later, a similar accident happened at a bungy business based in Germany with no connection to AJ Hackett Bungy. They had no pool beneath their tower and the customer fell to his death, showing how fortunate we were for having insisted that a pool be installed during the construction of the Bali site.

This situation came about because of a lack of communication between our different sites. Since then, we've consciously kept all lines of communication razor sharp, especially as far as equipment goes.

A few weeks later we had what was our most major safety incident at the Kawarau Bridge involving a client who was dropped from about 20 metres while he was being lowered after a successful bungy. It was a relatively simple error, for some unknown reason, the lowering line was simply not connected to the bungy, so when the shock cord was released after the client stopped bouncing he, along with the bungy cord, went straight into the river. We have highly trained staff everywhere and the raft operator was able to fish him out immediately. He was fine but the incident highlighted how we had to continually focus on cutting out human error.

The second incident at Queenstown came at Skippers Canyon

within a fortnight of the first and it was, without a doubt, the closest that we have ever come to killing someone. At Skippers, a strong Canadian lass fell about 55 metres into one metre of water. The webbing on her ankle harness went into a single screw-gate karabiner. As she jumped, the webbing flicked over the screw-gate and undid the karabiner. There's perhaps a one in a million chance that the karabiner could have been unlocked in such a freakish way. It was fine on the initial jump, and at the bottom as the cord fully stretched out, but at the top of her rebound the webbing passed over the now-unlocked gate of the karabiner and as a result she was completely released. And she fell. Boy did she fall. Thank God, she hit the water perfectly with her lower back hitting the water first and bearing the brunt away from her limbs and head. Unconscious and floating down the river, the crew recovered her and flew her to hospital by helicopter. She stayed there for about three weeks with a couple of cracked vertebrae and some cracked ribs.

For a few years at that time, all AJ Hackett Bungy sites outside of New Zealand had been using a second harness for back-up. At first it seemed a bit excessive to me, but clearly it was the weak link in our system and the only part without a redundancy factor built in. Then I saw that it was making customers feel a lot safer and I insisted that all our sites adopt it.

The perception of our product is that with one death, the industry balloon has popped; AJ Hackett Bungy is out of business. Supposedly people will lose faith in us, but I'm not convinced about that: I think we've proven the safety standards over two decades and that record will win out. But you still don't want to kill anyone. Everyone involved in AJ Hackett Bungy — from Queenstown to Normandy — is really proud to have got to the point we're at with no deaths. A 100 per cent safety record is pretty amazing. But if you look at scuba diving, rafting and skydiving as an example, they have regular fatalities around the world and business keeps on rolling.

When we're looking to open new sites or do business with anyone new to bungy, we have a simple mantra: two million jumps, zero deaths.

Forget skydiving, parapenting or white-water rafting — the fact of the matter is you're more likely to drop dead playing golf than taking part in what is considered an extreme sport as long as you do it with people who care and who know what they are doing.

Every bungy jumping accident has one common factor. It's a key component of the industry and something that — sadly — cannot be flushed out completely, no matter how many safety reviews, independent audits and equipment checks you put in place. The common factor? Human error. This starts at the top of any management system. I believe that what was happening between Henry and me upset the equilibrium of the business.

Rubber does not simply break. Karabiners do not simply come undone on their own. If you find there has been a broken rubber or an open karabiner, then a human has made a mistake — either by using the wrong equipment or by using it the wrong way, or, more importantly, not having an adequate redundancy system — a second harness at Skippers for example would have prevented the accident. On paper, bungy is failsafe. The physics of it measure up and the mathematics all make sense. The only variable is the human component. Our secret — the thing that has kept Henry and me at the top of our game as far as safety goes — is that we've always demanded the most stringent safety standards. Simple as that. Safety has to come before everything else.

In the early days we spent a lot of time doing cycle-frequency tests, learning how bungy cords changed with time and use. For several years, I was personally the guinea pig for any jump we tested — I would strap myself in and take a leap before any clients came on board. A lot of the other operators were involving public within weeks of getting a jump going. We actually found that the way the cords reacted changed considerably with more use. This was a crucial learning experience and fundamental to us running our business without causing too much carnage.

Throughout my life I've been pretty lucky with injuries myself. For a guy who spent his youth playing rugby, surfing, skiing, rock climbing and later inventing AJ Hackett gravity systems, I came through those younger years pretty well.

I've had my nose straightened because when I was a kid a mate accidentally dropped a metal grate in my face as I was clambering out of one of the drains we used to explore near my house. I went around for a fair old while with my nose out of shape until I had the money to fix it.

I also managed to face-plant myself into some guy's elbow in a schoolboy rugby game, picking up a blackened, dead tooth in the process. It was only a decade later when we were planning the Eiffel Tower jump that a woman from the company selling the media rights sat me down and told me that my black tooth wasn't very photogenic and would have to be replaced.

Yeah, I was pretty lucky as a kid — there was no major damage done. My brush with death was to come in Vanuatu.

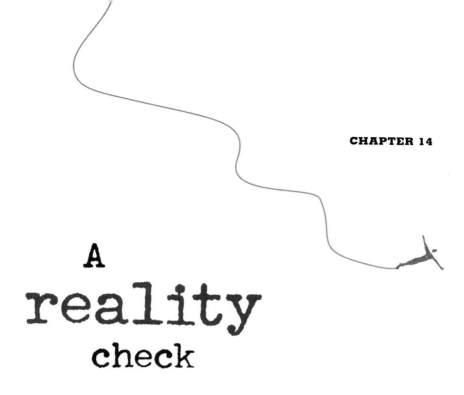

CHAPTER 14

A reality check

We get a lot of celebrity visitors at our bungy sites. Rock stars, actors, politicians, royalty and sports stars — they're all keen to take a tumble with some rubber around their ankles. But one day in the early stages of the Cairns operation, we had perhaps the most unique visitors possible. Two young men popped in from the original tribe of vine divers in the Pentecost Islands of Vanuatu. One of their tribal customs involves men and boys performing an annual vine dive, leaping from a wobbly tower with tightly wrapped vines lashed to each foot. Their vine jumping is the origin of modern bungy.

An Australian anthropologist called Murray Garde was spending about three months a year living with different tribes in the region and had developed close ties with the Pentecost

Islanders. He was acting as a liaison for these young men who had travelled to Australia to visit various Aboriginal groups. One day they were driving by the Cairns site and Murray said to his young guests: 'You guys might be interested to see this.'

Adam Lichtenstein was manager on the site at the time: 'It was amazing. I'd been working in the bungy business for almost a decade and you get to think you've seen most types of clients — the celebrities, the sports stars, people from every corner of the globe — then all of a sudden there's a young guy standing in front of you who is one of the hardcore vine jumpers. The originals. It was fantastic.'

Adam took them up the tower for a jump. They seemed shy and I expect that for these guys from the pioneering vine-jumping community, our modern bungy with its excessive safety procedures would have lacked a little frisson. But they loved it — there's no rebound on the vine jump and our tower in Cairns is twice as high as the peak of the vine-jumpers' tower, so it packed a bit of a punch for them. There is a little schoolhouse on the island and when they returned from Cairns half the village trudged a few kilometres through the hills to go there to watch the video that we made for them of the jump.

On the back of that impromptu visit, we hooked up with Murray Garde to find a way that we could have some involvement with the Pentecost Islanders. It was nothing major, but we felt that we could maybe do something for them. Murray helped us find an appropriate way to pitch in. Through Murray and the village head, Chief Telkon, we found out that the villagers had paid a deposit on a piece of land in Port Vila, the capital of Vanuatu.

It was pretty much just a shantytown but people from the island would use it as a sort of a halfway house if they needed to visit

Port Vila. A lot of the Pentecostal people had never ventured from the island but if they needed major medical help then a trip to Port Vila was the only way to go. For some of them, it is a first step towards engaging with the wider world.

People in developing countries are aware of the outside world, but the islanders are isolated from it and ignorant of its evils and problems. We brought two ideals to our thing with the Pentecost Islanders. One was preserving their way of living; keeping intact their mana, and the essence of the people and what they are about. A village is headed by a chief, who is often a smart guy, but they're getting constantly bombarded by Westerners looking to profit from them, to take something from them.

We've done well out of this bungy game and a lot of people around the world have loved it and had great experiences from it, but it all started in those islands and so it's only fair that bungy should do something for them. Secondly, we wanted to set them up so that people in the community could follow through with education outside of the traditional village confines, so they would then be able to preserve the village and the community's way of living with an awareness of how the world works.

We didn't want to simply dump cash on them, so helping out with their land purchase seemed like a good way to go. It was a way that modern bungy jumping could forge an understanding with the community that first developed it and put something back in for them. Murray Garde was instrumental in pulling the whole thing together. Affable and clever, we were so fortunate to have a guy who was deeply connected with the Pentecost Islanders on board and able to hook things together between us and them.

When the tenth anniversary of the Cairns site was approaching in 2000 we arranged for three of these vine jumpers to come over to be part of our celebration. They came and bungied in their traditional garb, which amounted to penis sheaths and not much else. We've had nude bungy jumpers from pretty much everywhere in the world, but these guys were particularly impressive. Physically they are all giants — taut muscles wrapped over lean frames — and the sight of them in traditional garb leaping from the top of the tower was inspirational.

Our links with the Pentecost Islanders cooled when the Cairns site went through a major directional change and today we're looking to rebuild some of those ties on a more permanent basis.

To find the reason for any stuff-up, don't look at the stuff-up itself; go back to the beginning. I nearly died in Vanuatu and that's a major stuff-up. I was making a world-first jump by doing a heli-bungy over the ocean and I hit the water bloody hard — the impact carried the equivalent of about a 40-metre free jump. It's the closest I've ever come to death and, without a doubt, the dumbest thing I have ever done in a lifetime of doing some pretty extraordinary things.

It was March 1993, and we had a deal to produce a series of action and adventure sports television programmes all based around Vanuatu. There was mountain biking (from the top of the volcano to the beach), filming the vine jumpers in action, my attempt at tropical heli-bungy and sports fishing. At the end of filming the action stuff, we were going to watch the vine jumpers. I flew directly from a company meeting in Las Vegas and, as usual after any decent company meeting, I was nursing an impressive hangover. By the time my flight reached Fiji, en route to Vanuatu,

I was tired as hell and nursing a nasty bout of flu to boot. In short, I was as sick as a dog.

I met Henry van Asch and Adam Lichtenstein who were helping me run the heli-bungy on the island in Vanuatu and we started setting everything up. We had some useful heli-bungy experience by then.

The original objective was for me to heli-bungy into the mouth of the island's volcano — just hold your breath to keep the noxious gasses out and everything would be all right. Sadly, weather conditions would not allow us to jump into the volcano, so instead we decided to go for a water touch from a heli-bungy, which had never been attempted before.

Adam Lichtenstein recalls: 'We'd done it [heli-bungy] in Queenstown and in Cairns, so we knew the deal pretty well. And, frankly, it's a pretty simple thing: you just have to watch your altitude and not make calls like the call we made that day in Vanuatu.'

We did one jump and everything went perfectly. I jumped from about 200 metres and the television cameras caught some great footage; so we headed back to shore and reviewed the successful jump. The helicopter was sitting on the beach and the bungy cord was laid out on the sand as we planned the next jump. I wanted to get closer the water, so that on the third attempt we could tune it right in and make the water touch, wrapping up this part of the filming.

I just wanted to get my work done so that I could crawl into bed, suck back some medicine and spend a couple of days recovering.

This was the first day of decent weather in a week, so everyone was keen to get as much shooting done as possible, but we were rushing things and I should have put my foot down right then. The first jump had been successful but there was some disagreement about how far clear I was from the water. I thought I was about 20 metres from the surface and the guys on the beach thought I was between 35 metres and 45 metres clear. I should have gone back and done the jump again from the same height to get a more accurate measure of how far clear I was. Instead we just rounded it up and said it was 30 metres clear. In my clouded, foggy state, I just wanted to get things done and wrap up before it got too dark.

'And you simply don't make a call on a helicopter jump like that,' says Adam Lichtenstein. 'With the cord being so long, it actually elongates further, even while it's sitting on the ground in the hot sun. It actually would have been up to a metre-and-a-half longer.'

The first jump had been from 200 metres and we decided to go down to 165 metres. Adam and another crew member called Moni fixed the bungy cord and Henry and I went up in the helicopter. And here's the biggest stuff-up: Henry and the pilot understood that the jump was to be from 150 metres. Perhaps the second-biggest stuff-up was that I was not able to see the altimeter from where I sat in the helicopter.

I wasn't on my game. When we did heli-bungy for clients, we checked every single thing in between every single jump; the cords were laid out and measured, the weights were checked and re-checked and every aspect of the flight was discussed with the pilot, even though it was a simple jaunt into the air. We would go away and debrief and make sure everything was as it should be. Somehow for this jump I let those standards slip when I was up there myself. The thing with a heli-bungy is that you have a massive variable: the helicopter. A little wind from the side, or a little down draft and everything changes. On a bungy site, it's easy to control a jump. If you want to touch the water, then that's no problem. A really good jump-master can control your jump so finely that they can get inch-perfect water touches. You get a little variation with how someone jumps off the platform, but by and large it's all knowable. It's simply not the same with a chopper.

Adam went on to manage a lot of commercial heli-bungy jumps. He says: 'To me it just came down to not making a call and saying: "No. We're not rushing this." We would never turn around a jump for a customer on such a short time frame, so we shouldn't have done it for one of us. But that's hindsight, and bravado, for you.'

There wasn't much bravado in me when I leapt from the helicopter and felt instantly that something was wrong. Henry, who was holding the cord clear for my downward leap, had released the cord a fraction late, so there was no sense of resistance against my harness — and you should feel some pull or resistance. This made me think there was something wrong with either the harness or the cord — that I was somehow unattached. In a split second I figured I was going to die, so I tucked my torso under to see what the problem was. If I was going to die, then at least I wanted to know what the problem was.

The moment I tucked my torso around, the cord kicked in, whipping me back and jolting my head downwards so that I was facing straight down again to be confronted with the next problem. The ocean. The water was coming up a hell of a lot more quickly than it should have been. I had barely enough time to get one arm covering the top of my head before I slammed into the water. It was like being hit by a truck. The cord still had vast loops and slack areas when I hit the water, it had barely broken my fall at all. My arm snapped immediately on impact, but at least it prevented my skull from cracking open and my neck from breaking. The impact also gave me a couple of compounded vertebrae.

I went in deep. I was completely buried down in the water to about four metres before the damn bungy cord whipped me out and jolted me around. Not the best way to administer acute medical care to a damaged vertebrae. Then, on my next drop, the cord belted me into the water again, so there I am getting dunked into the Pacific Ocean like a well-used teabag while waiting for the boat to come over and release me.

I was a wreck. The crew on the boat eased me down, and all I could think to do was ask for a cup of tea so I could collect my thoughts. Eventually, they took me to shore where the helicopter picked me up and raced to the airstrip so that I could be flown to Port Vila by aeroplane. Adam, Moni and Henry were left standing on the beach with the television crew and all the people involved with the other activities.

Adam tried to reassure the onlookers: 'Er, don't worry folks. I'm sure AJ will be fine.'

Lying on a stretcher in the helicopter, I promised myself right then that in future I would always have my top team around me for any extreme jumps.

That was an extra big portion of confront-your-mortality humble pie for me. I realised that the safety standards I insisted upon putting in place for customers and other jumpers were things that I had been brushing aside for myself. I had a young family that I loved very much and I didn't want to die. Hitting the water that hard hadn't killed me, but it made me reconsider my priorities, as many business affairs needed sorting out. What would have happened to my family if I had died that day? My interests in AJ Hackett Bungy were all held in trust, and there were no guarantees that Caroline and the kids would be taken care of. All of this was bubbling away in my mind a couple of years later, when Henry and I sat down to divide the company. I needed certainty to have peace of mind about the future of the people I loved.

Perhaps I should have been grateful. If the volcano jump had gone ahead and we had got everything so badly wrong, I might have been fried to a crisp.

It was a suitably chastised AJ Hackett, pumped full of painkillers, who returned to the Pentecost Islands the following day to attend the vine-jumping ceremony. I felt a bit of a dick; here were these guys jumping with nothing more than a penis sheath and a bit of a vine for safety and they managed to keep themselves alive and relatively unscathed, while I, with all the wonders of Western technology and medicine on my side, had almost managed to die.

Humbled and bruised, I was determined to witness the vine jumpers and pay my respects to the villagers. I returned to the island where it all began.

Vine jumping, or land diving, has taken place on the Pentecost Islands of Vanuatu for hundreds, perhaps thousands of years. Legend has it that a man called Tamalie mistreated his wife. Every time she ran away she was caught and punished until one day she fled to a tall banyan tree and climbed its branches with her husband chasing her up the tree. At the top of the tree, she taunted him, challenging her husband to get her and laughing at his cowardice. And then she jumped. Her husband, mortified, also jumped, not realising that she had tied vines to her ankles before she leapt. She lived; he died.

Her wit and bravery was celebrated annually with a vine jumping festival. Initially only women jumped, but as the years went by, men took over the jumping, perhaps to make up for Tamalie's failings. Eventually the jump came to mark the start of the yam harvest.

The vine jumping ceremony is a thing of wonder. The villagers spend ten days building a huge tower at the top of a steep slope in the jungle. The tower is divided into twelve sections, each representing parts of the human anatomy from the feet to the head. Then the men who will jump go into the forest where they choose their vines; each will choose his own, wrap it up and walk out of the bush. After that each jumper makes his own platform out of tough wood found in the bush. They whittle it down and chisel away at it, until they have sturdy platforms.

All the vines hang from the tower and this guy called 'The Doctor' comes along and looks at everyone's vines. He's a senior figure in the community, the big cheese when it comes to vine jumping — the ultimate jump-master. He takes a look at the vine and has a look at the jumper, then he feels the vine and closely inspects it. Then he pulls out a big machete and slashes the vine at the point from which it will be tied on to the jumper. It's an amazing process and the precise point at which the machete slash is made is based on years of experience. Every vine is going to have different qualities in terms of elasticity and breaking points and every vine jumper is going to be a different weight. Yet this guy — with no measures and scales and literally with the jumper's life in his hands as he swings the machete — makes all these calculations in his head. Inside the vine is all this stringy material and that's what is bound to the jumper's ankle.

The night before the ceremony all the jumpers sleep under the tower to ward off evil spirits. The spirit of Tamalie is in the tower until the jumps are completed.

On the day of the jumps, the parallels with the atmosphere on this tower and up a modern bungy tower are interesting, given that the two have evolved so separately. There's one person in charge: the jump-master. Up the tower they have a heap of guys getting the jumpers ready and checking everything over, just as we do. The jumper himself is a bundle of adrenalin and nerves — ditto.

But the mechanics are worlds apart. The main difference is that these vines are taut — this is no bungy operation, you don't get to bounce back up and wave to the camera. When you get to the end of our bungies, you are (relatively) gently hauled back into the sky. When you get to the end of a Vanuatu vine, your feet are yanked and your body whips around. You can see the shock of the sudden stop in the jumpers' bodies.

The tower in Vanuatu has a little bit of give in it, but not much. The jump platform, which the jumper has made for himself, is rigged up with a cross support beneath it in such a way that it snaps over the beam as the weight hits. As the vine goes taut, the platform snaps over the crossbeam and the tower takes on a slight lean. Young boys jump from the lower levels of the tower as their first step into manhood. From there, they move one level up the tower every year.

Immediately before a leap, the jumper will stand on his

platform and give a short speech about family matters, village politics or something that matters greatly to him. He can pull out at any moment without shame. Arms crossed over his chest, the jumper tumbles off the platform to a great cheer from below.

The vine jumpers aim for a slight ground touch. They're clever people so the surface immediately beneath the tower, where the jumpers hit the deck, is heavily sloped. This means if they come in too hard (and they all come in bloody hard), they'll be sort of angled off. The soil is dug up and turned so it makes for a slightly softer impact as well.

But make no mistake, the thing that keeps these jumpers alive is the bloke with the machete determining the length of the vine. These are incredibly brave men.

As rewarding and humbling as it would be to take part in this ceremony, I would never want to make this jump myself. As I understand it, no Westerner has made a vine jump in Vanuatu. And I hope none ever does — it simply wouldn't be appropriate. The thought of hundreds of Westerners trudging up into the Vanuatu bush to make this jump as part of the global adventure tourism circuit sends shudders down my spine. I would hate to think that what we've started with rubber bungy cords could lead to such a desecration of a noble traditional ritual.

Would I trust the bloke with the machete to get the measurements right? Why not? The faith his jumpers put in him is no different from the faith that thousands of people every month put into our business and our jump-masters. Just as I don't understand the process of how he figures out where to make that slash on the vine, those jumpers at AJ Hackett sites from Queenstown and Cairns to Bali and Normandy don't understand the process involved in what we do. You've just got to have faith.

CHAPTER 15

The **big** picture

Since we first opened for business, more than two million people have taken the leap at AJ Hackett Bungy sites around the world. Now I'd say that 99.9 per cent of those two million have been pretty happy with what they experienced. It sits in the top five of most people's list of major life experiences: losing your virginity, marriage, divorce, having a child, first hangover, getting sacked, blowing your first paycheck on a party . . . okay, maybe the top ten experiences.

We've created this unique challenge for our customers. The safety facilities are pretty much faultless, so the challenge is all in the customer's head. Every ounce of your being tells you that deliberately tumbling off a high platform is the wrong thing to do. Having the opportunity to overcome that natural reaction — that understandable recoil from a plummeting drop — is what makes bungy jumping such a special experience.

Simply put, there are two things that people know they are

getting into at an AJ Hackett Bungy site. Firstly, they know they are jumping with the safest operator in the industry — possibly one of the safest tourism operators in the world. Secondly — and probably most importantly in terms of marketing — the customers know that they are jumping with the original. We invented this game, we do it better than anyone else and we never miss an opportunity to remind the market of those two facts. Henry's staff in Queenstown, and my guys around the world, all offer the best bungy experience you can have.

It was securing the top-end of the bungy market and mastering the ability to deliver high quality in all aspects of the business — safety, merchandising, even the snack food available at the bungy sites — that put us in a position to last in the industry when all the dodgy operators have died away.

Often in this sort of business you get opportunists who come along when they see a fast buck. It's when things come back down to earth that you'll find the people who are worth dealing with. They're the ones who care about doing things right and are still around. We're long termers, that's why we don't mind losing the odd battle, because we win the war at the end of the day. There are very few businesses that work exceptionally well from day one and the people behind those businesses will operate at different levels of speed and patience.

My belief that bungy is simply too great to fail has given me a patience and a willingness to hang in there when some of the sites we have started didn't fire on all cylinders at once. I see the big picture. It helps that I'm a very laidback guy anyway. By 1992, when I won the Sir Jack Newman Award for individual contribution to New Zealand Tourism for the year, we were really starting to get somewhere.

Another strength which I like to think I have is that I'm a very good mediator. I surround myself with wild characters when it comes to doing business — I'm attracted to people who are willing to try interesting stuff, it's in the nature of my game. It generally takes a very level temperament to deal with all the dramas that these characters bring along.

The other thing I've developed over the years through dealing with these bungy sites and businesses around the world is the ability to come into situations, absorb what's going on quickly and then make a couple of big calls. Sometimes those calls create anarchy. In the short term it's sometimes difficult for the organisations and the people who work in them to cope with the reality of these calls, but it's good for them and the sites all grow out of it. I've done that with so many companies. I've become a doctor of fixing commercial stuff-ups.

What I've always set out to do with these bungy businesses is simple: create an opportunity for how things could be in an ideal world. Then I've accepted immediately that it's impossible for things to be perfect. I believe that driving any business is the same: the triumph isn't in achieving perfection (you never will), it's in staying on the road towards it.

Having me wander onto a site from out of the blue and create all that upheaval isn't easy on the staff. That's why our guys are a special breed and also why they tend to be a pretty colourful lot. Having the right staff is vital. As well as you think you know your business, the best staff should know it even better than you, at least when it comes to dealing with the small stuff, the day-to-day details; facing — and most importantly, understanding — the customers. If you're running a newspaper and you're a 60-year-old editor, and your journalists are all in their late forties or fifties, then your newspaper is going to have a certain perspective on things. It'll be a pretty conservative read and it'll engage with an older audience.

In the adventure tourism industry, the audience that we're typically engaging with is younger — a hell of a lot younger than me! — so it's always been crucial that we have a young, dynamic team working on our sites. We're pitching to backpackers and leisure travellers; people who are living pretty much a dream existence for a year or so, taking time out to bum around and do some cool stuff. Even the customers who aren't exactly in that backpacker demographic are buying into the lifestyle ever so briefly. You need to have staff who can identify with that. You can't manage this sort of team like you would an ordinary group of employees. When the occasion calls for it, I encourage the team to get out and party. You probably won't find many business management textbooks that urge you to have loads of young, single party animals on your staff. But in my business these guys and girls are out there acting as the face of the operation, getting more clients in the door the next day and — crucially — bonding among themselves.

The bond that our staff form over a few beers is crucial to the atmosphere on our bungy sites and the upbeat vitality of our organisation. Our staff are truly unique — most came into the industry first as customers, taking a bungy jump just like any one of the clients who steps up each day. Enthused, charged, fired-up, these characters get so high from a bungy jump that they turn up and ask for jobs. Our staff don't have to do bungy jumps, but pretty much all of them do.

I reinvented modern bungy jumping, I made my name and my business with bungy; but the immediate future for AJ Hackett International — and AJ Hackett, the bloke — will have a lot less bungy in it.

Essentially, I've boiled down the essence of bungy — that personal challenge that excites and satisfies so many people — and found new ways to take that challenge into new markets. We're not moving away from bungy, it's just that as we move into new markets, bungy is sometimes a bit too radical for them, so we're finding ways to take the core elements of bungy and bring it into people's lives.

Asia is the obvious market for us to grow into, although Asian markets can be a little wary of anything unconventional. We are starting to make inroads into these markets, with sites in Macau and Kuala Lumpur. Many large Asian cities have towers. What other people see merely as a structure for beaming out radio waves or an observation platform with a revolving restaurant, I see as an untapped adventure wonderland in a major city centre.

These towers make ideal launch pads for the kind of vertigo-confronting challenges that we set up with bungy two decades ago. Sky jumps, external tower walks and flying foxes are the way to develop these markets, without going too full on with the full bungy deal. I wouldn't rule out a regular commercial bungy from the towers in the future though.

Those sites on the tall towers are the changing face of AJ Hackett internationally; they're the way forward for us. You've got up to two million visitors a year visiting some of these towers anyway, so you don't have the same need for marketing to bring people to the site as you do with other locations.

And the towers are generally built in the heart of the city, so there's also a massive population right on your doorstep. With the benefit of hindsight, I know that managing my first bungy operation in France would have been easier if I had chosen a site on the outskirts of Paris, rather than in Normandy. In 2002 when I set up at the tower on Macau, near Hong Kong, I knew that I was onto a good thing. We've also just opened at the Kuala Lumpur Tower in Malaysia as well as a new venture in Panama where we operate a nightclub and adventure activities on the hill next to the canal. The challenge for me here is to broaden the demographic for the products we offer — taking our business from something that seems natural to 18–35 year-olds, to one that anyone from five to 80 will be excited by.

The companies owning towers in Kuala Lumpur, Macau and even Auckland want something original. The thing is, they've done what they do to death: there are only so many angles you can get on a revolving restaurant. And there are only so many people who are going to go up to the viewing platform and, lord knows, not many will come back for a second look. The companies may make a bit of money on telecommunications up top but once you've bought the souvenir and you've sent the postcard— what's next? That's why most of these towers actually operate at a substantial loss — the Eiffel Tower is the notable exception. If building one of these towers costs in the region of US$100 million, then you need to be making in the region of US$10 million a year just to get a return on your investment. It takes a lot of creative thinking to make money on that kind of scale.

That's where we come in. We provide something additional and unique for people to do at the tower site. A reason to stay and a reason to visit again. Our adventure sites bring repeat business and drive advertising possibilities and other angles for media exposure for the tower owners. Because the towers cost a lot of money, generally speaking the operators are open-minded about having other businesses involved with them that will bring in foot traffic. Clients walk over to watch a bungy jump and then eat in the restaurant or buy a souvenir.

As I proved in Auckland, towers are great for bungying, but aside from the Asian market's reluctance, we've also found that staffing sites there for bungy would be a problem — there's only a finite number of jump-masters in the world. Running a bungy operation requires some pretty full-on attention from some really onto it people — you have to be keeping teams of capable people well versed and able to run a site without killing anyone. That creates quite a big human resource problem. In running more basic personal challenge stuff at these other tower sites, the safety component is easier to take care of. It becomes easier to do short transfers and put people into new sites for a bit, while senior staff are freed up to deal with the big picture.

It's easy enough to get someone to move from New Zealand to France or Cairns, but once you're going into some of these other spots the whole thing can be a major cultural leap for some unworldly antipodean lad, so you have to be able to send the right people into these places. Without the right people on site, it's not even worth considering a bungy operation.

The Macau tower is a beauty. It's 340-odd metres high and at the base we have activities like a swing bridge, an adventure park, bungy trampolines and climbing walls. Then as you go up to the main observation platform of the tower, we've got the skywalk, where you can walk around the outside of the building. Challenges like this are all about exposure — there are no handrails or anything, you're just hooked on to a harness on your back, 230 metres above ground level. Then there's the skyjump — a freefall with a cable on your back with which you leap down to the ground. It's not a bungy, there's a propellor system that resists air and as a result stops your controlled descent just as you arrive on the ground. Then we also have mast climbs where you can climb to the very top of the mast.

The new project is to put in a giant swing at ground level; it's about 50 metres high and utilises the tower as an anchor for the cables. We are now setting up the highest commercial bungy jump in the world at 230 metres!

Macau has been the start of the process of getting into large towers around the world — the process is that you're inside the marketplace, rather than having to get people out to some distant destination. And it's Asia — there's more than 300 million people living within three hours' driving time of our Macau site, and within three hours' flying time there are three billion people. The Asian continent is big enough for these towers not to rub up into each other's markets. Kuala Lumpur is far enough away from Korea, and Shanghai is far enough away from Macau.

Developing the Macau and Kuala Lumpur sites has been fantastic. Seoul Tower is the next one we're looking at and, when that's under way, I'm going to make a big effort to go into mainland China, India, and possibly further afield to Russia. The key for me is to always have a well-connected local partner. The same applies for taking any business into a new country: know your trade and let your local partner know the locality.

So that's where my business is going. Where am I going personally? I'm going where my business is. There's a lovely corner of a small island off Lombok in Indonesia which I'm developing as a new home in the southern hemisphere. When it's completed, I'll live there in the southern winter months and scoot back to France for the skiing in the northern winter. This way I can be near my businesses in Asia as they develop.

This is a chance to get back into surfing Indonesian breaks, living in constant sun and warmth and many of the lifestyle things I've given away by living in the French Alps.

I've broken or held every record you can come up with in bungy at one point or another. I plan to celebrate the 20th anniversary of bungy in 2007 with a one kilometre plus jump over the Great Barrier Reef near our Cairns site. Once we break that one kilometre barrier, we could offer wealthy clients jumps from one to three kilometres.

I'm not that fussed about making any more big record-breaking jumps. I've had my fill of those and it would need to be something unique to get me excited. The world's deepest cave is 426 metres — Chris Allum had a permit to bungy into it in 1994 but two French base jumpers went before he could get organised. They used a helicopter to get out and the noise startled birds that nest in the cave, ruining their eggs, so Chris's permit was cancelled. That could be an interesting jump, I guess.

The fact of the matter is, I could bungy jump just about anything. You build it and I'll jump it. With the right crew around me, it's all a matter of logistics and planning. After two decades, we've got that down pat.

For sheer height, you could take a helicopter up to 10,000 metres and do a bungy jump for 3,000 metres — piece of cake. But what's the big deal? If you know all the cords are in good order and you've done all your homework properly then a big jump of that magnitude would really just be a matter of physics — and of course finding the cash to make the thing feasible. I get more personal satisfaction from a nice little jump — say 50 metres or 100 metres — where you can maybe touch the water, and get a good ground rush. There's nothing as invigorating as that sensation of the surface rushing up as the walls of a valley shoot past you. Now that's exciting.

The big deal for me now comes from facing the challenges of launching my business into Asia and expanding others around the globe, now that we have a solid presence in these markets. It's taken the best part of a decade for my international group to recover from the trauma of 'the Divorce' with Henry and the New Zealand sites, but recovered we have, and now my business can move boldly forward. I've built this bungy enterprise from nothing twice and I'm ready to continue building.

Well, I hope you had as much fun reading my first book as we all had putting it together. It was a hard job trying to fit everything we wanted into the book so as a bonus, we've put some additional material on our website for you to check out. You'll be able to see movies and photos of things I describe in the book.

To see clips and photos of some of the jumps I've described in *Jump Start* head to *www.aj-hackett.com* and go to the *Jump Start* link, follow the prompts and enjoy!

Don't forget, *Challenge Life, Challenge Yourself*, and we look forward to seeing you at one of our sites soon!

AJ Hackett, August 2006

AJ Hackett International Bungy Sites

AUSTRALIA
AJ Hackett Bungy Cairns
McGregor Road, Smithfield
PO Box 700, Smithfield QLD 4878
Australia

Bookings: +61 (0)7 4057 7188
Freecall: 1800 622 888 (Aust only)
Fax: +61 (0)7 4057 7003
Email: bookings@ajhackett.com.au

FRANCE
AJ Hackett Bungy France
Viaduc de la Souleuvre
14350 La Ferrière Harang
Normandie
France

Bookings: +33 (0)2 31 66 31 66
Fax: +33 (0)2 31 66 31 67
Email: info@ajhackett.fr

GERMANY
AJ Hackett Bungy Germany
Sports Unlimited

Lichtenau

Kohlstatt 7

D-86706 Lichtenau

Germany

Bookings: +49 (0) 8450 - 92 38 92

Fax: +49 (0) 8450 - 92 30 73

E-Mail: info@sportsunlimited.de

INDONESIA
AJ Hackett Bungy Bali
Double Six Club

Blue Ocean Boulevard

Legian Beach

Bali

Indonesia

Bookings: +62 (0) 361 731144

Fax: +62 (0) 361 730466

Email: bali@aj-hackett.com

MACAU
AJ Hackett Bungy Macau

Adventure Zone

Level T2

Macau Tower

Macau

Bookings: +853 9888 656

Email: ajhackett@macautower.com.mo

MALAYSIA
AJ Hackett Kuala Lumpur

Kuala Lumpur Tower

No. 2 Jalan Punchak,

Off Jalan P. Ramlee,

50250 Kuala Lumpur,

Malaysia

Bookings: +603 2020 5145

Fax: +603 2098 8308

Email: info@ajhackett.com.my

NEW ZEALAND

AJ Hackett Bungy New Zealand

The Station – Queenstown Bungy Centre

Cnr Camp & Shotover St

Queenstown

New Zealand

Bookings: +64 (0)3 442 4007

Freecall: 0800 286 495 (NZ only)

Fax: +64 3 442 4907

Email: bungycentre@ajhackett.co.nz

Acknowledgements

AJ

My loyal best mate and sister Elaine; Granny Joe who is the coolest mum on the planet; Adam Lichtenstein, Mike Champoux, Christian Ferrier, Adam Quinn, Luke Johnston, Charlie Bassett, Stefan Roux, Berty, Pierre, Ryan, Hippy, Henry van Asch, Chris Sigglekow, Chris Allum, Jonni Deaker, Andy Brinsley, Nigel Hobbs, Mike Newberry . . . thank you so much for your guidance, faith, trust and commitment and for putting your balls on the line with me.

For all the clients that have stretched their minds to bury fear for that special moment and opened up to living life to the max — charge on! — and a huge thank you.

There have been heaps of people involved in helping this book end up in your hands. Winston Aldworth has worked with me to turn my words into this book — thanks mate. I'd also like to thank Jenny Hellen and the team at Random House for their work. Thanks again to Chris Sigglekow for the photos.

Cheers to all my crew, past and present, and other mates who've helped to make my life the ride that it's been. There are too many of you to name but you know who you are! Most of all I'd like to thank my family for their patience and support.

Winston

I would like to thank the following people: Bronwyn Sell, Jenny Hellen, AJ and the Hackett whanau, Andy Brinsley, Hippy, Andrew Potter, Louise Taylor, the legendary crew at the Palace Backpackers in Brisbane, the first-rate stars of the Brisbane police force and the countless mates who pitched in, gave tips and bought rounds. Cheers.